Caring

*How Can We Love
One Another?*

Morton T. Kelsey

PAULIST PRESS
New York/Ramsey

Acknowledgements

Material from *Marriage: Dead or Alive* by Adolf Guggenbuhl-Craig is used by permission of Spring Publications. The excerpt from *The Wounded Healer* © 1972 by Henri J. M. Nouwen is used by permission of Doubleday & Co. Inc. Material from *The Jerusalem Bible,* © 1966 by Darton Longman & Todd Ltd. and Doubleday & Co. Inc. is used by permission of the publishers. The quote by Jacob Needleman from "The Tao—Illumination and Corrections of the Way" is used by permission of *Theology.* Material by Catherine of Siena from *Western Spirituality* is used by permission of Bear & Company, Santa Fe, N.M. Material from *Meister Eckhardt* is used by permission of Harper & Row, Publishers, Inc. The excerpt from *Today's English Version of the New Testament* © 1966 by the American Bible Society is used by permission. Material from The New English Bible © 1961, 1970 by the Delegates of the Oxford University Press and the Syndics of the Cambridge University Press is reprinted by permission. Excerpts from *The Lion, the Witch and the Wardrobe* by C. S. Lewis, © 1950 by Macmillan Publishing Co. Inc., renewed 1978 by Arthur Owen Barfield, and from *The Betrayal of the Body,* © 1967 by Alexander Lowen, are used by permission of Macmillan Publishing Co. Inc. The excerpt from *Memories, Dreams, Reflections* by C. G. Jung, recorded and edited by Aniela Jaffé, translated by Richard and Clara Winston, © 1963 by Random House, Inc., is used by permission of Pantheon Books, a division of Random House. The table from *On Being a Good Listener* is used by permission of Forward Movement Publications, N.D., 412 Sycamore St., Cincinnati, O. 45202. The quote by Rudolf Steiner from *Knowledge of the Higher World and Its Attainment* is used by permission of the AnthropoSophic Press. The quotation by Will Durant is used by permission of *Parade.* The quotations by C. G. Jung from *Modern Man in Search of a Soul* and from *The Little Prince* by Antoine de Saint Exupery are used by permission of Harcourt Brace Jovanovich Inc. Material from *The Collected Works of St. Teresa of Avila,* translated by Kieran Kavanagh, O.C.D. and Otilio Rodriguez, O.C.D., are used by permission of I.C.S. Publications. Quotations by St. Augustine from *The Good Marriage* are used by permission of The Catholic University of America Press. Material from *Emotional Development and Spiritual Growth* by Timothy J. Gannon is used by permission of Franciscan Herald Press. The quote from *The Road Less Traveled* © 1978 by M. Scott Peck is used by permission of Simon & Schuster. Excerpts from *After the Fall,* © 1964 by Arthur Miller, is used by permission of Viking Penguin Inc. Excerpts from *The Face Beside the Fire* by Laurens Van der Post are used by permission of Hogarth Press Ltd.

Library of Congress
Catalog Card Number: 80-84659

ISBN: 0-8091-2366-5

Published by Paulist Press
545 Island Road, Ramsey, N.J. 07446

Printed and bound in the
United States of America

Contents

To my wife Barbara
and my children
Myra, Chip and John,
who more than any others have
taught me what loving and caring
are really about

Preface

For many years I have been fascinated by the mystery and power of love. These reflections have been many years in forming. The importance of love was poignantly apparent to me since childhood. However, the cosmic significance of love only began to emerge clearly as I tried to present the Christian message in three different churches over thirty years.

Nearly every week during this period I had to produce a sermon on some subject relevant to the life and needs of the congregation. As a pastor I came to realize that there was no subject more crucial and important than the nature and practice of loving and caring. These sermons gave me the opportunity to present various aspects of this central reality of Christian life to my listeners and myself. The sermon is often more valuable to the preacher than to anyone else. Over the years I wrote several dozen sermons on the various aspects of the mystery of love.

In the late 1960's I was invited to give some talks at the Church Divinity School of the Pacific, and I gathered these sermons together into a coherent whole. Later this material was mimeographed so that those who heard me lecture on the subject of love might have something to mull over after I was gone. One of these mimeographed papers came into the hands of David Garaets, the Abbot of the Benedictine monastery in Pecos, New Mexico. The press at the Abbey, Dove Publications, printed these reflections in a pamphlet, *The Art of Christian Love*.

In late December of 1975 I was asked to give a retreat at the Abbey on the subject "How Can Christians Love One Another?" In the midst of this community I gave fourteen lectures. My wife and I agree that the community at Pecos is trying as sincerely and consciously to express the idea of Christian love as any group of people we know. In that atmosphere I found myself saying things which I had never said before. These lectures were taped, and a year or so later my friend Margie Grace had the lectures transcribed from the tapes. This book presents in written form the essence and implications of what I presented in those talks.

I have learned about love in four ways. First of all I learned from Jesus of Nazareth and the church which has falteringly tried to express his love over the centuries. However, I did not fully understand what the church was saying until I came into a dead-end street and entered analysis. Here I experienced with Max Zeller and then with Hilde and James Kirsch the meaning of unconditional caring and concern. We cannot truly know love until we have experienced it. What an incredible joy it was to be able to share all of myself and find no rejection or judgment. Max Zeller's family saw what Max gave to his clients. A friend reported to me that his ten-year-old son was once asked by a friend what he wanted to be when he grew up, and he replied without a moment's hesitation, "The patient."

As soon as I began to bring some order into the chaos of my own life, a strange thing happened. People began to knock at the door of my office and wanted me to listen to their fears and confusion. I discovered that I could pass on to other people the unconditional acceptance I had received. I learned an incredible amount from those who came to me for understanding, acceptance and Christian guidance. It is one thing to show unconditional love for an hour within the framework of the counseling situation in my office. It is, however, quite another to try to express the same kind of love to those with whom I live twenty-four hours of the day. And it has been my wife and children who have shown me more than any others what is required if I am truly going to be a loving person.

All this time I had been reading the Bible and the lives of the saints. The more I experienced love as a counselee, as a counselor, and as a husband and father, the greater the depth I found within the Christian heritage. I found many new insights in that heritage and new ways of expressing love in all my relationships.

During this same period I immersed myself in the writings of modern psychology and depth psychology in particular. Sometimes I found greater emphasis on the value and necessity of love in this secular tradition than I found among the writings of contemporary theologians. The followers of Freud saw *eros* as central to human fulfillment. Sandor Ferenczi made it the keynote of his writing and practice. Izette de Forest has described Ferenczi's great contribution to psychoanalysis in her excellent book, *The Leaven of Love*. Erich Fromm wrote his influential book, *The Art of Loving;* and Milton Mayeroff published a magnificent anatomy of love in his book, *On Caring.*

In most of these secular, psychological studies of love, however, there is a scornful indifference to the question: How does love fit into the fabric of the universe of which we are a part? Among the secular psychologists only Dr. C. G. Jung and some of his followers have seen the spiritual, divine implications of love. Jung wrote that in earlier times love or *eros* was seen as a god and that we cannot understand it unless we still see its divine significance. However, Jung was a disillusioned minister's son and so he usually turned a blind eye to the value of the specifically Christian world view as an aid to the understanding of the nature of love.

Classical, orthodox Christianity and secular psychology have much to offer to one another. They say many of the same things and they can help each other in avoiding errors and stupidity; they enhance each other. They each support and clarify what the other is trying to express. And yet I have seen no attempt to bring these somewhat hostile siblings to reconciliation. One basic purpose of this book is to present an integration of the insights of both fields. In his book *The Road Less Traveled* M. Scott Peck has worked toward this integration. His discussion of love is one of the finest I have read, but his theological understanding leaves something to be desired.

The subject of love is central to the teachings and life of Jesus of Nazareth and to the Christian Church. I have written several books about various aspects of Christian life and practice. There will be, quite naturally, some repetition here of what I have written elsewhere. However, this book is written to answer the very practical question which most people ask sometime in their lives: How can we love one another? Many of the answers come from my own fumbling attempts to answer this question for myself, and so this book is very personal. It is the sharing of my own search.

As I continued on my journey toward the meaning and practice of love, more and more suffering people came to me to unburden themselves. A large number of them were having problems in loving and being loved. Like the hero in Charles Williams' novel, *All Hallows Eve*, many of them cried out: "Why isn't one taught to *be* loved? Why isn't one taught anything?"[1]

It became clear that we human beings do not know instinctively how to love one another. We need to learn how to be loved and how to love. I began to study and work earnestly in order to understand the complex subject of human relationships. We developed a clinic at St. Luke's Church where I was rector, and I was licensed as a Marriage, Family and Child Counselor in the State of California. I became a member of the American Association of Pastoral Counselors and the American Association for Marriage and Family Therapy. For nearly twenty years a major portion of my time has been spent listening to people talk about the things which were bothering them. Top on the list of problems was the inability to love and to feel loved.

In every meaningful hour spent with counselees I learned as much as they.

*   *   *

I wish it were possible to give credit to all those who have contributed to the insights which appear in these pages. The list would be ridiculously long, for it would include nearly everyone who has truly touched my life. In addition to those whom I have already mentioned, there are a few to whom I owe special gratitude.

Caroline Whiting has worked with me on several manuscripts. She read the original transcript from Pecos very carefully and offered many suggestions which I have incorporated.

Three friends have particularly contributed to my understanding of love. Dr. Leo Froke led me into many avenues of psychology I might not have otherwise explored. John Sanford and I have discussed the subject of this book and its specific implications in my life on innumerable occasions. Andy Canale and I have dialogued on most important subjects and on the subject of love in particular. Another friend, John Whalen, edited the finished manuscript.

Richard Payne, my friend and editor at Paulist Press, urged me to put top priority on writing these reflections; and I am grateful for his encouragement and wisdom.

My wife Barbara has given me more consistent love than anyone in my life. Our relationship has provided many of the insights which come from living in the tensions of honest human relationship. In addition she has demonstrated that love by listening many times to lectures on this material. She has listened to the manuscript after it was written. She has spent hours going over the typescript and making additions and corrections as well as checking references and reading proof.

I am also grateful to Rosalind Winkelholz who has put my incomparably bad typing into a readable manuscript.

1

The Centrality of Love

As the years have passed I have become convinced that love is the central reality in this universe of ours, and that our primary task as human beings is to know this love and to express it to those around us. Paul stated this idea incomparably in the first letter that he wrote to the Corinthians. Unless our lives express the quality of self-giving caring, we have little significance or worth. Unless our religious gifts, our alms, our knowledge are exercised in love, they have no value and we are nothing.

I had often read these words and I knew that they were central to Christianity, but they did not come alive for me until I understood how they applied to me concretely and specifically. I know the very moment that they became luminous with meaning for me. I was flying home from a conference which I had led in North Carolina. I was flying Piedmont Airlines and so had an imminent sense of eternity. I was alone, quiet, turned inward, reflecting in my journal.

First of all I realized that we were flying not too far from the home of my brother with whom I was not in good relationship. I then observed that the next lap of the journey would take me not far from the home of my father and stepmother with whom I was not in very good relationship. And then I would be flying to see my teenage daughter in Phoenix, Arizona. I was stopping there on the advice of a friend who suggested that perhaps I could mend our relationship if I visited her on her home territory at college. Our communication had just about broken down as she came to the conclusion that being a clergyman's daughter was a fate little better than death. At fifteen she informed us that she was an atheist and didn't want to go to church any longer. I am grateful that my wife and I had the wisdom to know that if we had not made a positive impression upon her by that time, forcing her to go to church would certainly not produce it.

Sitting in the quiet, mulling over this tally of spoiled family relationships, some words bubbled up from the depth of me. Had someone asked me if I knew these words, I would have said that I did not; but some secret recess of my psyche had registered them and brought them up at the right moment. The words were those of *A Simple Prayer*, often attributed to St. Francis:

O Divine Master, grant that I may not so much seek
to be consoled . . . as to console,
to be understood . . . as to understand,
to be loved . . . as to love.

And then, there in the silence of the plane, wave after wave of insights broke over me. I realized how much more interested I had been in receiving consolation, understanding and love than I had been in giving them. If brother, parent or child did not give me what I needed, then the relationship had failed. I shuddered within myself. I realized that the basic problem in the parish was the same; most of us were more interested in being treated like Ming vases than in caring for others. I realized that emotional maturity only *begins* in us human beings when we begin to give consolation, understanding and love without expecting anything in return. The essential mark of true adults is

2

their ability to give of love without looking for what they can get back.

In that moment on the plane I also understood for the first time that we cannot follow Jesus of Nazareth and his way until we find it more important to give understanding and love than to receive them. As we give up our desire to be consoled and understood and loved, we die in a very real sense and something new has a chance to live and grow within us. If we continue on this way, we lose our lives in order to gain them. We die and rise again. This is the creative way of the cross which any of us can follow. As we try to live by this insight, the whole gospel begins to make sense. It opens up like a tight bud. The meaning of the Christian way becomes clear.

The validity of these insights was confirmed before the day was out. The plane landed in Phoenix. I was determined that I would try to express a new kind of love toward my daughter, yet I was dreading the visit as much as she was. Later I found out that when I called to tell her that I was coming to visit her, she had turned to her best friend and said, "What on earth will I do with Father for five hours?"

She met me in the friend's car (obviously a clergyman's daughter could not afford one). I asked her where she would like to go to lunch, saying that I would take her anywhere. She had not often been treated in this manner by her father and could not think of a place to go; I took her to the nicest place I knew, the Arizona Biltmore. We had lunch by the pool, the waiters hovering over us. Suddenly I was seeing her as a real person, with real needs, not just as *my* child. Something of my new attitude must have broken through to her. Quite tentatively she asked me if I would like to go shopping with her in the Thomas Mall that afternoon. Although that was not exactly my idea of a Saturday afternoon in the lovely Arizona February, I paused to reflect before I answered. I thought to myself that I was not there to be taken care of but to love. And so I replied quite honestly that I would love to go shopping with her in the mall.

3

We walked up and back the interminable length of the mall several times. I was aware of Myra and her reactions just as if she had been a sensitive and hurting counselee. I noticed that our pace slackened in front of a shoe store, observing that her eyes were focusing upon a pair of yellow shoes. I asked her if she would like to try on those shoes, and she replied that it would be a nice idea. Naturally they fit perfectly. This is known in theological language as divine providence. There was a yellow bag to match and I asked her if she would like to have that, assuring her that these gifts would not come out of her allowance. She thought the bag would be nice, too.

Something happened between us that day. Myra realized that I could treat her as a person in her own right and with love. From then on neither of us dreaded our getting together. It was no longer "What will I do with Father for five hours?" but "Why don't you come more often and stay longer?" I call this experience "the sacrament of the yellow shoes." Myra has since married and has children. Her life expresses a fine understanding of the meaning and practice of Christianity and Christian love.

From every side I began to receive additional evidence that love is the secret motive force in human destiny. I never know when or from what source I will find another confirmation of this truth. In spite of the fact that the secular world seldom professes much belief in the power or practicality of love, we do find telling examples of its effects now and then even there. The following example comes from one who had studied history and certainly had no religious axe to grind and was published in *Parade* newspaper magazine on August 6, 1978.

After spending a lifetime studying and writing about men and events, historian-philosopher Will Durant, 92, has distilled more than 2,000 years of history into three simple words: "Love one another."

"My final lesson of history," says Durant, "is the same as that of Jesus."

"You may think that's a lot of lollipop," Durant adds with a laugh. "But just try it. Love is the most practical thing in the world."

History has taught Durant to be "realistic" about human nature. "I accept man as history shows him to be: good and bad, competitive and cooperative. The best I can do is take human beings as they are and assume that they are going to be decent, and I find that if I make that assumption, it helps them to be decent.

"If you take an attitude of love toward everybody you meet, you'll eventually get along." . . .

"In any generation," says Durant, "there may be eight or ten persons who will be 'alive' in the sense of continuing influence 300 years after. For instance, Plato still is, Socrates still is."

But in all of Western civilization, the person who stands out above all others, says Durant, is Christ. . . .

No one portrays human life more realistically than Shakespeare. He knew our human hearts. Jung once said in reference to Shakespeare that he also knew God. His comedies and tragedies reduce human existence to the level where we can comprehend it and deal with it. The stories of jealousy and anger with which these comedies and tragedies begin are not very different. But there is one crucial distinction between the tragedies like *King Lear, Hamlet,* and *Othello* and the later comedies such as *The Winter's Tale, Cymbeline* and *The Tempest.* In the tragedies, at the critical moment, the characters do not express self-giving love and the forgiveness which always accompanies love. In the comedies love and forgiveness are present at the critical moment and tragedy is avoided.

The Paradox of Love

A friend of mine, Robert Johnson, wrote me a Christmas letter which has meant a great deal to me over the years. He suggested first of all that the mystical experience was as much present among men and women today as it had ever been. He then went on with these words: "The finding takes only simplicity and directness. The simplicity yields that most simple statement possible from Scripture: God is love. Directness takes one to search for the experience of love within one's own life." He then went on to write that we can only find the full splendor of God as we come to know what love is concretely, in our own lives.

Yet most of us are afraid to love, and there are good reasons why we are afraid; and he continued, "With love there are no defenses, and we may be hurt deeply, again and again. And then, as we truly love, the power and majesty and splendor of God come upon us, and this is not always gentle or easy to take. The splendor of God has little in common with a Sunday school picnic, or the parlor game of love. When we allow ourselves to love specifically, fully and consciously, concretely in depth, then we come to the very edge of Love itself (love with a capital L); we come very close to the mystical splendor of God. From many sources we are told that the mystical splendor of God will first burn us down, melt away all that does not belong to us, shear us of everything that we thought necessary for life, destroy everything that is not pure gold in us. . . ."

St. Teresa of Avila continually reminds us of the transfiguring, painful ecstasy of the encounter with "His Majesty" as she calls the Divine Lover. Most of us know that such an experience is not an easy one. But this may be the most important experience in life, and probably the only human experience that is eternal and cannot be lost in the shuffle.

Trying to manifest love in my life has been no easy task and has involved me in endless paradoxes and questions, conflicts and joy. Several years ago, while talking with my good friend, John Sanford, about the mystery of human life and human love, he made a statement that I will never forget: "I know a good bit about sexuality. I know a good bit about transference (falling in love). And I know something of love. However, when I add all of this together I know absolutely nothing."

Jung expressed much the same idea at the conclusion of his autobiography written in the last years of his life. He

6

stated his belief that the human capacity to love was as important in understanding the nature of the universe as was rational reflection. He went on: "I have again and again been faced with the mystery of love, and have never been able to explain what it is." He concludes that the human being "can try to name love, showering upon it all the names at his command, and still he will involve himself in endless self-deceptions. If he possesses a grain of wisdom, he will lay down his arms and name the unknown *ignotum per ignotius* (the unknown by the more unknown)—that is, by the name of God. This is a confession of his subjection, his imperfection, and his dependence; but at the same time a testimony to his freedom to choose between truth and error."[1]

Before I write another word, let me express clearly and emphatically that I am only a beginner in the art of loving. As I have meditated on the subject of love and as I have tried to embody it, I too have found it mysterious and incomprehensible. It is only with fear and trepidation that I undertake to write on the subject of love and caring. But in spite of my inadequacy and limited understanding I feel that I would be more remiss not to try to describe what I have experienced than to do so in a halting manner.

Human life is an organic whole. I have discovered no way in which I can separate my prayer life from my practice of caring for other human beings. Prayer which does not result in others feeling more loved by me is hollow and flat. My efforts at love which are not inspired and sustained by an experience of the grace of God usually come to nothing. I become more and more convinced that human love which does not reach beyond the boundaries of this mortal existence is satisfactory neither for the realization of my own potential nor for the support, development and actualizing of the person I would love. It is difficult to understand genuine, self-giving love without some experience of the love of God and the prayer and meditation which so often lead to that experience.[2]

The reader may object that we have not yet defined love, have not described exactly what we mean by love.

This is true, but love cannot be defined in neat categories and simple logical propositions. Sitting in our leather chair in our study and *thinking about* love will not reveal its nature.

M. Scott Peck gives one of the best descriptions or definitions of love that I have encountered, one that springs out of his many years as a practicing psychiatrist. He believes that psychotherapy is seldom successful unless genuine love is expressed between the therapist and the client. He writes:

> I am very conscious of the fact that in attempting to examine love we will be beginning to toy with mystery. In a very real sense we will be attempting to examine the unexaminable and to know the unknowable. Love is too large, too deep ever to be truly understood or measured or limited within the framework of words. I would not write this if I did not believe the attempt to have value, but no matter how valuable, I begin with the certain knowledge that the attempt will be in some ways inadequate.
>
> One result of the mysterious nature of love is that no one has ever, to my knowledge, arrived at a truly satisfactory definition of love. In an effort to explain it, therefore, love has been divided into various categories: eros, philia, agape; perfect love and imperfect love, and so on. I am presuming, however, to give a single definition of love, again with the awareness that it is likely to be in some way or ways inadequate. I define love thus: The will to extend one's self for the purpose of nurturing one's own or another's spiritual growth.[3]

Love is an experiential reality. We have either experienced it to some degree or not. We have either known what it is to be loved and to love, or we know a little or nothing. Those of us who have never known what it is to be loved or have never tried to love others can no more de-

8

fine what love is than the blind can hold forth on the many shades of red. If we have not had some experience of love we cannot tell what it is any more than we can describe the taste of fresh crackers and blue cheese unless we have munched on that delicacy. We need to experience love if we are to know it and talk intelligently about it. And incidentally, if we would know God, we had best seek until we discover the experience of love; none of us can know or love God until we have experienced love to and from our brothers and sisters. Love can also be described by its results, but we shall defer describing the results of love until later.

No reality or existence, not even mathematical reality, is exhausted in words of definition or description.[4] Anything which really exists needs to be examined from many different perspectives and even then the best of descriptions cannot encompass it completely; however, we do the best we can, hoping that others will fill in important data where we have omitted it and correct us where we have been mistaken.

Something as simple as the relation of one electron to another cannot be fully and adequately described, nor do we understand how one simple amoeba relates to another. How much less can we understand and fully lay bare the incredible complexity of two human beings in their deepest and most complete interchange. Love is a complex and amorphous experience that penetrates every aspect of human existence. Its different aspects overlap and intermingle. As Jung has suggested, we say either too much or too little. The subject is so vast that I could easily write a book on any one of the following chapters, and so I limit myself, knowing that I will not say enough. On the other hand, as we try to describe love we will inevitably seem to be saying the same thing several times. There is no way of avoiding some repetition as we try to do justice to the subject of love.

We will look at the subject from many different angles and consider it in many different ways and tell stories about love. The nature of love may then reveal itself in the same way that shy people may reveal themselves when the conditions are right. A strictly logical discussion of love and caring would probably not be worth the paper on which it was printed. Let us begin by turning to story as an introduction to the mystery of love.

2

Love and Story

There is no greater human need than to love and be loved. This need touches the deepest level of the human heart. And the need to love may be deeper and more central than the need to be loved. Often we receive our meaning from our loving actions toward others. Laurens Van der Post expresses this truth superbly in his novel on the nature of love, *The Face Beside the Fire*. Speaking of the lives of his characters set against the background of primitive Africa, he writes: "For do we not all know, in our aboriginal hearts, that the tragedy of the individual is not so much not being loved as being unable to love, as if by some dark impediment which seems to cut us off from the full rhythm of life?"[1]

I have been listening to people for thirty-five years; and when we get beyond the superficial questions and fears, longings and doubts, I find that most women and men are seeking to be loved and to love. I remember one college student in particular who came to talk to me. He seemed to have everything going for him. He was intelligent, good looking, a fine athlete, and had many friends. After a dozen sessions together he finally revealed his deepest fear. He wondered if he was capable of truly loving any other human being.

Nearly all the great religions of humankind speak of the importance of love, its vital significance. Buddhism tells of the Boddhisattvas who deny themselves the bliss of Nirvana in order to return to help others find this release and fulfillment. This action is particularly admired because it is not the logical consequence of enlightenment. Many Hindus worship the savior god, Ganesha, who is the heart and soul of compassion. They want little direct contact with Shiva and Kali, the primordial masculine and feminine deities. Indeed they do not even like to mention Kali by name. The followers of Islam are constantly referring to Allah as the all-merciful and compassionate. Works of charity for the poor and for slaves are highly recommended in the Koran. Many of the Sufi saints speak of a mysticism of love. In Taoism and Confucianism men and women are not following the Way or Tao if they are not compassionate or caring. The I Ching speaks again and again of the creative life which is characterized by quiet, humble, unobtrusive concern for others. Judaism has grown and developed over four thousand years of its stormy history. Few discussions of the value and importance of love are more profound than those of Hassidic Judaism.

And yet, while all this is true, no great religion places love as consistently in the center of its thought and practice as Christianity. Being a human institution, the church has often failed to live up to the message of its founder and its scripture; and so-called Christian culture is far behind the church. However, where Christians have lived close to the spirit of Jesus of Nazareth they have been called saints; and the chief characteristic of their sainthood has been their knowledge of God as love and the expression of that love in their lives through concrete actions of compassion and caring.

The Centrality of Love in the New Testament

One could write an entire book on the importance of love in the Old and New Testaments. Our purpose, howev-

12

er, is the practical one of trying to discover how we can love one another as Christians. There is little question that love was considered central by Jesus of Nazareth and by those who were closest to him, as well as by those who have followed him most closely through the centuries. Let us look once again at some of the central passages in the New Testament about love.

One passage to which I return again and again in the Gospel of John summarizes discipleship. Jesus says: "A new commandment I give you: love one another. As I have loved, so must you love one another. If you have love for one another, then all will know that you are my disciples" (John 13:34–35). The essential distinguishing sign of being a follower of Jesus is found in manifesting or showing forth the kind of love and caring which Jesus had for his disciples. In a passage from the Sermon on the Mount Jesus extends this love to all human beings and distinguishes his teaching from that of the Old Testament. "You have heard that it was said, 'Love your friends, hate your enemies.' But now I tell you: love your enemies, and pray for those who persecute you, so you will become the sons of your Father in heaven. For he makes his sun to shine on bad and good people alike, and gives rain to those who do good and those who do evil" (Matthew 5:43–45) It would be difficult to make love more central to the human condition than this.

The New Testament letters give the same message in characteristically different words. The author of the First Letter of John writes: "God is love, and whoever lives in love lives in God and God in him. . . . If someone says, 'I love God,' but hates his brother, he is a liar" (1 John 4:16, 20). The author of the First Epistle of Peter writes: "Above everything love one another earnestly, because love covers over many sins" (1 Peter 4:8). And Paul is constantly talking about the centrality of love. Not only does he write a paean or hymn of praise about love in 1 Corinthians 13 which we shall discuss later, but in his letter to the Romans he writes: "Be in debt to no one—the only debt you should have is to love one another. Whoever loves his fellow man has obeyed the law. . . . To love is to obey the whole law" (Romans 13:8, 10).

13

Wherever the Christian church has been vital there have been saints who lived and spoke of love. In the prayer attributed to St. Francis (and certainly epitomizing his life) we find these words: "O Divine Master, grant that I may not so much seek to be consoled as to console, to be understood as to understand, to be loved as to love." St. Catherine of Genoa in her highest prayer experience of Jesus Christ and God would murmur quietly, "Oh Love, oh Love, oh Love." She and her followers attempted to bring this love to the rich, the poor and the condemned. St. Catherine of Siena was asked by one of her nuns how she could show God how much she appreciated all the blessings which she had received from him. St. Catherine replied that it wouldn't do her any good to indulge in more fasts and vigils or to build a magnificent temple. But she could find someone as unworthy of her love as she was of God's love. Then she might show that person the kind of love which God had shown her. In this way she could show her appreciation. There are hundreds of saints who speak the same basic message.

In the Old Testament we find the same emphasis on love, although it is not the central focus as in the New Testament. Hosea takes a prostitute as his wife and forgives her again and again as a living symbol of God's enduring love and patience for his people Israel. In Genesis Joseph forgives his brothers who have sold him into slavery. David is characterized by his love for those around him. God goes along with Abraham as he asks for mercy if only ten just people are found in Sodom and Gomorrah. In Leviticus we are told to love God and our neighbor as ourselves. Jesus picks up this theme of love found in the Old Testament and makes it central to his teaching and practice.

The Meaning of Love

There are few words in the English language which are more ambiguous than "love." The word can refer to a passionate desire which is largely physical lust, or to the possessive love of a parent which can stifle and destroy a child. It can refer to the love of friendship, the love of brother and sister for each other, or to romantic love. The word can even be used in scoring for tennis. The Greeks had many different words to describe the different kinds of love. In English the word "love" is used to describe all of the nuances of positive human relationship, and so we must be quite careful to show what we mean by love or we can shed more confusion than understanding, more darkness than light when we talk about love.

The love that we are talking about refers to that complex of emotions, attitudes, movements of will and actions in which we reach out to others in a caring, concerned manner, desiring to let other people know that we care about them and wish to facilitate the achievement of their potential. My love is never complete until the other person feels more loved by me. Love is my total behavior (emotions, feelings and actions) directed toward making another person feel more cared for by me and by the Divine Lover who is at the heart and center of the universe.

The love of which the New Testament and religious people are talking can be described as that kind of caring concern for other human beings which is interested in enabling others to come to wholeness and fulfillment as human beings and so achieve their eternal destiny. This love stops at nothing, never gives up and is best exemplified in the love which Jesus of Nazareth, Jesus the Christ, has shown for lost and confused humankind. Many people equate love with their feelings of love. They think that it is intransitive. It is just a personal feeling and does not necessarily need to carry over to the other. The love I am describing is not satisfied just being an emotion. It is transitive. It continues to love other human beings until they feel loved. I am not loving merely when I feel loving, but when others feel loved and cared for by me.

If love were merely personal emotions and feelings, God might have looked down upon earth where miserable human beings were struggling in confusion and fear and hatred and said: "Tough luck. They are having an awful time. Poor miserable wretches, how I love them." God did more than that; he saw the agony of human beings, and when he could not get his message to humankind through

15

the prophets, he came as a human being at Christmas time to reach us where we are. He reached out to others even on a cross until they finally allowed themselves to be loved. God's action is the perfect expression of love. It is a mixture of concern, caring and action. When we love we participate in God's way of reaching out to humankind.

Love really cannot be understood unless it is illustrated, and it is best illustrated in story. Most important ideas cannot be defined in rational concepts. They can best be described in stories, in myths, in word pictures, in symbols. Jesus often spoke in story and parable. Most of us human beings resort to story when we wish to talk of important things dealing with meaning and value, with death and eternal life. One basic idea of Christianity is that God could only get the message of love across to human beings as he became a living story in the fabric of history. Story is often helpful when we wish to communicate important matters.[2] And so let us turn to story for an outpicturing of love.

After the Fall

Significant stories are often autobiographical. Our first story about love is taken from the play, *After the Fall,* by Arthur Miller. Twice he had failed in loving and he wondered if he were capable of love. His second marriage was to Marilyn Monroe. He found that he was not able to truly love her.

The play describes the gradual disintegration and dissolution of their relationship and love. Marilyn Monroe brought to the stage her own wistful, haunting, broken, hurting spirit which was crying out: "Can anyone really love me?" Her tragic suicide resulted at least in part from believing that no one could ever understand, care for her, love her. Most redblooded men in America thought to themselves: "Just give me an opportunity and I'll show her love." This made her a sensational box-office attraction. Arthur Miller had the opportunity and failed. No wonder he questioned his capacity to love.

The play itself is fascinating; the stage depicts the mind, and people pop up and down on the stage just as

16

thoughts and memories do in the human mind. As in a reverie there is no logical time sequence, yet the story unfolds with clarity. In the play Quentin, the character who represents the author, meets a European woman, Holga, who has survived the bombings of the Second World War. They are having a picnic outside a Nazi concentration camp. Indeed, the stage directions suggest that the backdrop portray just that. Such misery is often the backdrop of the human soul.

As Quentin and Holga begin to relate to one another, he discovers that she hopes, even after all she has been through. Holga has been through hell—not the hell of a "natural" catastrophe, but the hell we human beings make for one another in war. He questions her, asking how she can hope after all she has been through; and she replies, in one of the wisest passages in modern literature.

> "Quentin, I think it's a mistake to ever look for hope outside of oneself. One day the house smells of fresh bread, the next day of smoke and blood. One day you faint because the gardener cut his finger off; within a week you're climbing over the corpses of children bombed in a subway. What hope can there be if that is so? I tried to die near the end of the war. The same dream returned each night until I dared not go to sleep and grew quite ill. I dreamed I had a child, and even in the dream, I saw it was my life, and it was an idiot and I ran away. But it always crept onto my lap again, clutched at my clothes until I thought, if I could kiss it, whatever in it was my own, perhaps I could sleep. And I bent to its broken face, and it was horrible ... but I kissed it; I think one must finally take one's life in one's own arms, Quentin."[3]

I have been told that Arthur Miller married this Austrian woman and they had children, the first a beautiful child and the second defective. This passage is not just sentiment. Arthur Miller knows what it is to love the idiot, outwardly and inwardly. Perhaps this is why the passage rings with such authenticity.

17

Toward the end of the play, Quentin begins to catch the secret of hope and love. Still puzzling over how Holga could hope and love after all the horror and pain and agony she has experienced, he cries out:

"Or is that exactly why she hopes, because she knows? What burning cities taught her and the death of love taught me: that we are very dangerous! And that, that's why I awake each morning like a boy—even now, even now! I swear to you, I could love the world again! Is the knowing all? To know, and even happily, that we meet unblessed; not in some garden of waxed fruit and painted trees, that lie of Eden, but after, after the Fall, after many, many deaths. Is the knowing all? And the wish to kill is never killed, but with some gift of courage one may look into its face when it appears, and with a stroke of love—as to an idiot in the house—forgive it, again and again ... forever?"[4]

And often the second inner person we confront when we turn inward with honesty is the inner murderer. I have come to trust only those people who are aware of their inner murderer. I have come to trust only those people who are aware of their inner rage, of the inner murderers within them capable of murdering me. Only those who know their capacity to destroy can keep it in hand and deter it. Tertullian wrote that only the Christian truly knows the devil. If we are to love others it appears that we must know and love ourselves, even the destructive and idiotic parts of us.

A Strange Ceremony

Often we do not realize the strange quality of the New Testament. We become numb to it by familiarity. Just before Jesus was captured by the authorities and brought to trial and death he met with his disciples for a last supper. It was the day before the feast of the Passover. The disciples did not expect anything unusual. Jesus had warned them, but they did not hear him. They were chatting with one another, discussing the stories Jesus had told and the incredible power that he displayed.

Suddenly Jesus got up from the couch on which he was reclining, took off his outer garment and wrapped a towel about his waist. Then he took a basin and water and began to wash his disciples' feet. Such an action would be considered eccentric if it were to happen in a modern setting with a religious leader and the group of his intimate followers, but it would not have produced the shock that it created for these Semites. The foot was considered one of the most disgraceful parts of the human body. Among modern Mideastern peasants it is still impolite to speak of the foot without saying "Excuse me." The feet of those who walked through the streets of Jerusalem were stained with sewage and offal. Only the lowliest servant or slave was given the task of washing the feet of the household or of guests.

This kind of action by a religious master is still uncommon, as one can witness who has seen the Zen *roshi* being waited upon by adoring disciples. They carry footstools and cushions. How different this action of Jesus was from that of the Hindu swami who is preceded by young men and women scattering flower petals before their master.

At first these disciples were so dumbstruck that they did nothing. They just submitted, almost in fear, certainly in consternation. Then Jesus came to Peter, who was able to blurt out in his characteristic manner: "Are you going to wash my feet?" Jesus replied: "You do not know now what I am doing, but you will understand later." And Peter protests: "You will never at any time wash my feet." Jesus then told him that he would have no part of Jesus if he did not allow him to wash his feet, and Peter cried out, "Not my feet only but my head and my hands also."

How many times Jesus had told them that the Son of man came not to be ministered to, but to minister, and that he was among them as one who serves. But it took this dramatic enactment of service, this footwashing, in order to drive home his message and meaning. And then he explained his action to them "I am your Lord and Teacher and I have just washed your feet. You, then, should wash one another's feet. I have set an example for you, so that you will do just what I have done for you." Then he went on to tell them that his only new commandment for them was that they love one another as he had loved them. This is the kind of caring and love that Jesus was constantly proclaiming.

In many churches one often finds sentimental pictures or stained glass windows of the good shepherd carrying the lost sheep back to the sheepfold. Sometimes we are almost embarrassed by this sentiment, but it certainly portrays the spirit of Jesus in looking for the lost, whether it be a sheep or a lost coin or a soul. I have often wondered how many times Jesus told these stories for his hearers.

And then Jesus tells the utterly absurd story of the prodigal father and his stupid, wayward son. After arrogant and profligate debauchery in which he breaks the moral law, he then breaks the ritual law by feeding swine. When he can stomach this no longer and his belly is pinched with hunger, he goes home and there is received with love, mercy, compassion, a feast and the best brocade robe. He is even given the signet ring which welcomed him back into full legal sonship. And the prodigality of the father does not cease with this. When the older brother comes in from the fields and hears the music and dancing and sees his home blazing with burning torches, he refuses to come in, and the father, in a way totally uncharacteristic of the Semitic peasant, goes out to plead with his spiteful, arrogant, self-righteous son, begging him to join them. One cannot discuss the nature of love without referring again and again to this central story of Jesus as Kenneth Bailey points out so well in his book, *The Cross and the Prodigal.*

Jesus gave the same message repeatedly in other stories and aphorisms. He told of the laborers in the vineyard who came in late in the day and received the same wage as those who had worked all day, because they needed that much in order to live, and the master was merciful and loving. The compassion of the Samaritan to the Jew who was a deadly enemy is another example of the same theme. The

Jew would have crossed the street to avoid the Samaritan and would have spat at him had he come close; and yet the Samaritan bound up his wounds, took him to the inn and paid for his keep until he was well. How magnificently these stories illustrate the words of Jesus found in the Sermon on the Mount: "You have heard that it was said, 'Love your friends, hate your enemies.' But now I tell you: Love your enemies, and pray for those who persecute you, so that you will become the sons of your Father in heaven."

Jesus explained that the reason that we should be loving is not only for the good it creates and the joy it brings, but because by loving we share in the very nature of God himself. Love is the very warp upon which the fabric of the universe is woven.

What Jesus expressed in word and story and illustrated in the footwashing, he expressed most completely in his willingness to be crucified and rise again in order to give assurance that love is eternal and immortal and that those who share his life and spirit can be lifted out of themselves, transformed and brought to eternal life. This was Jesus' supreme story, the story of his death and resurrection which he lived out. The followers of Jesus never really understood the secret of his life until after his death and resurrection. Paul writes in his Letter to the Romans: "When we were still helpless, Christ died for the wicked, at the time that God chose. It is a difficult thing for someone to die for a good person. But God has shown us how much he loves us; it was while we were still sinners that Christ died for us! By his death we are now put right with God. . . . We were God's enemies, but he made us his friends through the death of his Son. Now that we are God's friends, how much more will we be saved by Christ's life" (Romans 5:6–10).

Nothing better illustrates the love of God, the centrality of love in the very structure and grain of the universe, than this death and resurrection. There is no way in which this truth could be expressed in logical propositions. It needed the story that Jesus lived as well as the stories that he told in order to get this message through to his disciples and to us.

A Fairy Tale

In order to understand the true significance and meaning of Christian love it is helpful, if not necessary, to become like young children once again. And sometimes when we listen to a children's story, a fairy tale, we can share in the child's openness and wonder. C. S. Lewis has written a modern fairy tale which expresses better than anything else I know the essential meaning of the Easter story, the Christian story. My daughter was only twelve when I first read her *The Lion, the Witch and the Wardrobe.* When I finished reading the story to her, she said (and with no prompting from me): "Father, that is the story of Jesus and Easter, isn't it?" But let's get to the tale itself.

Four children in wartime Britain are boarded in the country in an old and rambling house. They discover a wardrobe in one of the rooms through which they can pass into another dimension of time and space, into Narnia which is ruled by the White Witch. She is the epitome of evil and under her rule it is always December and never Christmas. One of the children, Edmund, turns traitor over some candy and betrays the others to the White Witch.

All is lost until Aslan, a numinous lion, appears and rescues the country by his power. However, he cannot save the traitor, Edmund, except by offering himself as a ransom for him. And so Aslan dies and Edmund is set free. It seems as though the end to all hope has come when Aslan is destroyed. However, there is a deep magic from beyond the dawn of time which states that those who give their lives for others, expecting nothing in return, cannot really die. The lion, Aslan, rises from the dead.

> There, shining in the sunrise, larger than they had seen him before, shaking his mane . . . stood Aslan himself.
>
> "Aren't you dead, then, dear Aslan?" said Lucy. . . .
>
> "Do I look it?" . . .
>
> "But what does it all mean?" asked Susan when they were somewhat calmer.

"It means," said Aslan, "that though the witch knew the Deep Magic, there is a magic deeper still which she did not know. Her knowledge goes back only to the dawn of Time. But if she could have looked a little further back, into the stillness and the darkness before Time dawned, she would have read there a different incantation. She would have known that when a willing victim who had committed no treachery was killed in a traitor's stead, the Table would crack and Death itself would start working backwards. . . . "[5]

The power of this story is strange indeed. For many years I taught a graduate class at the University of Notre Dame entitled "Death, Dying and Suffering." In it we explored the meaning of death and evil. After reading Menninger's *Man Against Himself* and Elie Wiesel's *Night, The Lion, the Witch and the Wardrobe* was assigned to counteract the ugliness which these other two books conveyed. Reading this fairy tale would almost always dispel the darkness. Reading the gospel story would not have done the trick—the students were immune to that.

One year a graduate student in psychology was taking the course. Lewis' book made such an impression that she dreamed of a magnificent medallion head of Aslan. She drew what she had seen. Her husband worked in stained glass and executed the dream-vision into stained glass. They gave it to me as a token of gratitude. The story of Aslan and his sacrificial love had opened the doors of belief for her again. Those portals had been closed to her for several years. The meaning of Easter and Christ touches me as well in a new way each time I see the sun streaming through the glass medallion into my living room.

A Story of Betrayal

In *The Seed and the Sower* Laurens Van der Post tells one of the most moving stories that I have ever read. It is the story of two brothers. The elder brother was strong, tall, intelligent, an excellent athlete and good student. Sent away to a private school in South Africa where he lived, he

23

quickly made a name for himself. He became an admired leader of the student body. His brother was some six years younger. He was not good looking or capable, and he was a hunchback. But he had one great gift. He had a magnificent voice and could sing like a nightingale. I found it easy to identify with this story deeply as I was such a younger brother (even though I couldn't sing).

Eventually the younger brother joined the elder at the same boarding school. One day in a cruel mob action typical of adolescent and crowd mentality the student body ganged up on the younger brother, mocked him, abused him and tore off his shirt to reveal his hunchback. As so often happens, they projected upon this strange and different youth their own inner idiots which they sought to destroy in hurting him.

The older brother was aware of what was going on. He could have gone out and faced this mob of cruel, sadistic students. One word from him would have put a stop to the whole spectacle. He was a leader. He could have acknowledged the strange one as his brother, but instead he remained in the chemistry laboratory doing his work. He betrayed his brother by what he failed to do. Is not the ultimate in betrayal the refusal to go out with love when the other needs us?

The brother survived, but was never the same again. He kept to himself and no longer sang, returning home to the family farms. Meanwhile the elder brother had become a soldier in World War II, stationed in Palestine. One night, lying outdoors gazing into the starlit night, he realized what he had done to his younger brother in their school days. His heart told him that he would never have peace until he went home and asked his brother for forgiveness. And so he made the incredibly difficult wartime journey from Palestine to South Africa and met his brother. They talked long into the night. He confessed how he had betrayed him by what he had not done. They cried together, embraced, and the breach between them was healed.

Something else happened that night. As the elder brother was falling asleep, he heard the beautiful voice of his younger brother singing once again.

24

Van der Post writes that the task of every human being is to make the universal, concrete; the general, specific. By engaging in a concrete act of contrition, the elder brother acted out his love for the younger and thereby released each of them from his emotional prison. By his concrete act of caring he brought healing and wholeness to his brother, to himself and to the relationship.

The ultimate betrayal of life may well be the failure to love when one has the opportunity to do so. To speak of our universal love without living out specific actions of love may be the worst hypocrisy. If there is a sin against the Holy Spirit, it may be failing to express concretely and specifically the love which rises in our hearts.

A Homely Story

Love is not only concrete, creative and sacrificial; it is also conscious; its eyes are open wide. A friend tells this story:

"My sister and I shared a painful silence that expanded to fill the whole Datsun as we drove home to the suburbs from Chicago. Without meaning to, we had reactivated old wounds and started replaying old memory tapes. The feeling of sibling rivalry had been sparked off by an incident at a downtown restaurant. Being the more extroverted of the pair, I had dominated the conversation. Beginning to pick up on the non-verbal signals sent my way by the three other group members, I realized too late that once again I had easily slid into being the center of attention, leaving my younger sister to feel dull and unexciting by comparison. How well I knew her feeling, having fumbled my way through dinner parties where everyone's verbal brilliance had left me feeling particularly undazzling.

"Haltingly we began to explore our moods of hostility and resentment toward each other. 'You always take over; you're always the star of the show.'

"I listened to her barrage of accusations, trying to understand her feelings without losing touch with the validity of my own: 'I'm a natural extrovert; I'm not *trying* to outdo you.'

25

"Slowly the accusations died down and the hurt little girl feelings emerged. It was not an easy fifteen miles as we sought to really hear each other, to say to each other that we cared enough about being sisters to bother dredging up the sludge that seems to settle into familial relationships.

"What we discovered was that on the other side of the painful exploration we made was a deeper relatedness and love that we could never have touched if we had subscribed to the belief that love is without conflict. So often Christians have been guilty of preaching a brand of painless love that doesn't bring healing; rather, it buries resentments deep inside us where they fester and erupt months or years later."

A Concluding Story and a Beginning

Francis Thompson's poem "The Hound of Heaven" images God as the relentless seeker of human beings. Thompson was a derelict, a drug addict lost in the underworld society of Charing Cross, London. Still God pursued him. Eventually Thompson wrote a poem about the love which Mary, the mother of Jesus, had for all human beings, and he sent it to Alfred Meynell, the editor of a leading Catholic periodical. Meynell recognized a searching spirit in the poem even though it was scribbled on dirty pieces of scratch paper. He published the poem and sought out the author. He and his wife took Thompson into their home and then sent him to a monastery where he was rehabilitated. God sought Francis Thompson directly and through the love of the Meynells, and he became one of the greatest religious poets of the nineteenth century.

How often most of us flee from the love of God, from the Hound of Heaven. Whenever we stop and turn to God we realize that before we dreamed of turning to him, he was there reaching out to us. These words of the poet reverberate within the depth of us when we really hear them:

I fled Him, down the nights and down the days;
I fled Him, down the arches of the years;

26

I fled Him, down the labyrinthine ways
    Of my own mind; and in the midst of tears
I hid from Him, and under running laughter
    Up vistaed hopes I sped;
    And shot, precipitated,
Adown Titanic glooms of chasmèd fears,
    From those strong Feet that followed, followed
        after.
        But with unhurrying chase,
        And unperturbèd pace,
    Deliberate speed, majestic instancy,
        They beat—and a Voice beat
        More instant than the Feet—
'All things betray Thee, who betrayest Me.'[6]

In the matter of love God is the initiator; we are the re-spondents. Seldom can we offer to others much truly self-giving love until we have received it from the Divine Lover in one way or another. This takes us to the subject of how love fits into the fabric of the universe and how it seeks us out.

How do we know that God seeks us out? How can we be sure that he is the loving pursuer? Christianity claims that God became flesh in a particular Jew of Nazareth, a Jew living in the time of Augustus Caesar. God broke into human life in the person of this man. There are those who maintain that God did indeed break into time and history then, but that he no longer touches our lives directly. If Christians are to give a central place to love in their experience and in their theology, they need to have a coherent world view that enables them to believe that the nature of God is love and that this God and his kingdom can be known and experienced here and now.

We turn now to examine the theological bedrock—the belief system and world view—upon which the dedicated practice of love is based.

3

The Theology of Love

Human beings are more consistent than we ordinarily believe.* If we do not see how love is related to the central meaning of the universe, or if we doubt that there is any essential purpose there, we are not likely to place a high priority on our loving. Unless we believe that love and caring go along with the grain of the universe, we are not likely to continue in these ways of living and acting, particularly when the going gets rough. When we are pressed to the wall with fear and its companion, anger, it is difficult to maintain a loving stance unless we are convinced that this course of action has ultimate significance.

In order to love in a truly long-range and consistent manner, we need to think as well as to have emotions and sentiments, good intentions and strong will. It may be possible for the individual to have a strong personal faith and

---

*The reader who wishes to get on with the practical suggestions on loving can move on to Chapter 4 and go on from there. If, however, we are to have an understanding of Christianity's unique contribution to the centrality of love in human life, we need to come back to this chapter at the conclusion of the book.

even a vital prayer life without doing much thinking. It is next to impossible to communicate this faith in love and prayer as a personal relating to Divine Love unless we see where love fits into the total picture of things, into a world view.

If we wish to share the belief that love is central to the universe, we need first of all to witness to our experiences of love and to allow loving action to flow through us. We cannot convert anyone to love except by loving, as I have tried to show in my book on Christian education, *Can Christians Be Educated?* But in addition to this we need to care enough about other people to understand what they are thinking and why. We need to understand why they can't or don't believe. In order to do this we may find it necessary to do some thinking and see how love fits into our view of the world. Talking about love without using careful thinking can often degenerate into sentimentality and romantic drivel.

When we are frightened by the disbelief or agnosticism of others it is usually an indication that we are not very clear or secure in our own belief. Seldom are we secure when we have not thought through our convictions. Carl Jung once remarked that it was strange how Christians treat agnostics, ostracizing them and treating them as if they have a communicable plague. He went on to say that when we are truly confident of our own point of view the people most likely to intrigue us Christians would be the agnostics or atheists because we can show them the reality that they have overlooked and are missing. Personally I find nothing more challenging than agnostics and atheists; they have wrestled with the problems and are ready for an answer. The average conventional Christian is apt to be much harder to touch because he remains blissful, inconsistent and unreachable. As a pastor I used to say, "Give me a vociferous atheist and I will make him senior warden of the parish in five years!"

There are three essentially different ways to look at the universe in which we live. There is the view current among most people who have been touched by the materialism and rationalism of the Western world. It states quite simply that we live in a purely physical universe, and any idea of a spiritual world is illusion. On the other hand there is the view which is most common in Far Eastern countries and held by most Oriental people in one form or another. More human beings subscribe to this vision of reality than to any other. It states a diametrically opposed point of view. In this world view the physical world is illusion and the spiritual world is real. A third view dates back to our primitive human roots. It was the view of nearly all primitive religions, of shamanism and of Plato. It was also the view of Jesus Christ, of the Early Church (when Christianity was most vital), and of Dr. C. G. Jung. It is very difficult to make love the central orgainizing reality in one's life unless we have opted for the third view. Let's look at the reasons for this statement.

The Theology of Western Materialism

There is a common point of view lying beneath the thinking of most Western people (educated or semi-educated) in Europe and their relatives throughout the world, in New Zealand, Australia, South Africa, the United States, Canada, and Spanish America. It is quite simple. This belief system states that this world and the human beings who inhabit it are simply a complex arrangement of atoms or atomic particles. The human being is entirely limited by his five or six physical senses and any talk of being able to perceive or intuit anything beyond the purely physical universe is unthinkable. We are totally encased in a physical space-time box. According to this view, obviously there is no afterlife as we are only a complex pattern of particles; and when this complex system breaks up in death, the individual fragments then become part of another system of particles. Any reported experiences of the deceased are old wives' tales since such things are impossible.[1] When we are dead, we are dead and this is the end of us. Human value and significance ends with the grave. Any discussion of a spiritual element in human beings or of a spiritual world in which they can participate is pure nonsense, in both meanings of that word.

30

This view of the universe may be pictured with a simple diagram. The central box is the space-time box which exhausts all reality. It is purely physical. The little triangle represents the human being who is able to perceive through his five senses and then process this material through the intellect. It is difficult to explain how human consciousness arose in a physical universe. Perhaps it was a fluke. If one is a behaviorist one solves it by denying the reality of consciousness and seeing it only as a complex of conditioned responses. Outside the box there is nothing but the great void.

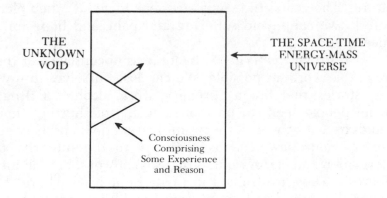

Where do love and God fit into this picture of reality? Quite simply, they don't fit at all. What are we most likely to observe when we have no conviction about reality other than that which is presented by our casual sensory look at the world? We are apt to see only war and chaos, muggings and cruelty, violence and the power play, murder and bloodshed, bickering and hostility. It seems that only power is significant in our world, the law of the sharp tooth and the tearing claw. Any honest reading of human history reinforces this observation. Any meaning we find in life we must make for ourselves, for this world of ours is only a meaningless collage of valueless bits and pieces.

There are four different ways to deal with a world like this. First of all we can play the power game. We seize as much power as we can. If we can do it legitimately, fine; if not, we will do it by any means we can. This is the way of the professional criminal. Hitler exemplified it better on a large scale than any other modern man or woman. When we find defeat inevitable, then we bow out in suicide. Naked power is amoral and so is living according to power. Those who essentially are seeking power are living nonmoral lives.

Another way of dealing with a meaningless universe is to forget it all and get as much pleasure as we can. We may develop the cruder pleasures of lust, violence and gluttony, or we can cultivate the more sophisticated tastes. In the latter case we become connoisseurs of wine, race horses, Middle English philology, symphonic music or Persian miniatures. The goal is the same—we seek to get as much pleasure as we can, avoid suffering and pain, and hope for a speedy end.

A third way is trying to become as unconscious of this miserable world as possible. We can lose ourselves in mystery stories, meditation, sexuality, work, alcohol or drugs. Some people seem to be more capable of shutting their minds to reality, while others simply can't do it and become anxiety neurotics. It is a testimony to the integrity of clergymen and clergywomen that so many of them fall into neurosis. They are trained in many seminaries where the materialistic view of the universe is held unconsciously by most of the professors; and their collapse is inevitable if they are truly very sensitive people.

The fourth method of dealing with this bad situation is heroism and tragic irony. Where there is no meaning, it is up to us human beings to make it for ourselves. Most secular advocates of love and caring simply tell us that the sensible and most satisfactory (even the most ultimately pleasurable) way of living is to live the way of love. This is the way of maturity and fulfillment even though it is snuffed out and comes to extinction at the grave. It is still good in itself and can utilize our full capacities. However, I have found very few human beings who are captivated and inspired by this prospect. Most people need to see more rootedness in love before they give their all for it. I have not observed that living love necessarily produces pleasure. Often it is a way of intense suffering as it was for Jesus and Socrates. Those with religious conviction about love and God were often able to stand up to the power creed of Hitler. The humanists, whether journalists, professors or scientists, in most cases capitulated.

These secular exponents of love perceive no way that we human beings can get any boost from anything beyond ourselves to invigorate and strengthen our capacity to love. Likewise they do not believe that there is any downdrag in the universe which inhibits and decreases our capacity to love. There is no inner murderer within us. Much of what these writers say is true. They often describe what love is and is not, quite accurately, but they seldom deal with the problem of why it is so difficult to love and why so few of us succeed in our attempts. In a purely physical universe there is no good or evil. There is simply that which is. Human beings make value. The problem is that most people with this point of view opt for one of the first three alternatives rather than the fourth. I know of no convincing argument or way of persuasion within their world view to get them to change their behavior.

Erich Fromm, however, does offer a theory of why things are so bad. He follows the thinking of Marcuse and Marx and Hegel. He believes that it is our bad economic system which creates the situation which makes it so difficult for us to love. It dehumanizes us. Marxism states that we are part of an inevitable historical process through which humankind must develop. It springs out of the very nature of physical reality and passes through the stage of capitalism which will finally be overthrown by a dictatorship of workers and will lead to a utopia in which each of us will produce according to our abilities to the limit of our capacities. Anyone who truly believes this religious creed will be inspired with enthusiasm and will use any means to obtain this goal. It is obvious that it is difficult for blasé materialists to do battle effectively with this creed.[2] There is some truth in this point of view. However, if it is hard for me at times to swallow the Christian story, it is ten times more difficult for me to swallow Karl Marx whose thought is based on questionable philosophic speculations and not even on empirical data. His thinking runs counter to all my deepest experiences.

33

The Tradition of the East

There are many more human beings who accept the Eastern picture of the universe than the Western one. This view presents a sharply contrasting picture of the world in which we live. It can be pictured simply in a diagram.

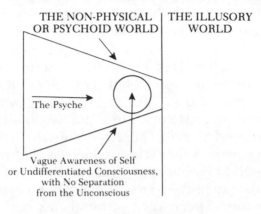

THE NON-PHYSICAL | THE ILLUSORY
OR PSYCHOID WORLD | WORLD

The Psyche

Vague Awareness of Self
or Undifferentiated Consciousness,
with No Separation
from the Unconscious

The physical world is illusory and the spiritual world is real. Specific human personalities are expressions of eternal spiritual realities within the unreality of the physical world and so they are also unreal. The clear distinctions between subject and object and the vivid perceptions of the physical world are the creation of the ego and are illusion. As one becomes enlightened, these distinctions and perceptions become blurred and disappear. The goal of human life is detachment from the *maya* of unreality, losing one's sense of ego and merging into the absolute. Human emotions like love and hate and fear tie one to illusion. The mature person becomes essentially emotionless.

The life process is understood as essentially circular or cyclical. Everything returns again and again to the static perfection of spiritual reality and then spins out into illusion *(maya)* once again. There is no meaning to history or to time, no purpose or goal to achieve. Through reincarnation everyone receives exactly what he or she deserves, for the universe is completely just. As the soul matures it comes finally to that state of non-personhood where one is no longer drawn into *maya* and one is free to merge into the imageless bliss of Nirvana.

34

What place does the love which we have described have within this picture of reality? It has little or none. The specific individuals around us are as illusory as we are, and we shouldn't waste our time on illusion. Loving acts of charity for specific human beings in their sickness or tragedy, in their poverty or grief, are also considered illusion. Such actions may even be detrimental, since they may decrease the karmic value of the just suffering that these people endure. Because of these acts of kindness, the individual may have to come through the cycle of reincarnation at the same level once again. Our task is to realize the illusory nature of existence, become detached from it and be able to get off the world. A trip through India some years ago made clear to me why Buddha wanted to get off the world with its teeming millions. The situation there, with the poverty and sickness and hunger, does appear impossible and insoluble.

The only charity is to help people to find the way out of illusion. It is for this purpose that the Buddhist saints, the bodhisattvas, return to earth. Acts of charity are like tears lost in the ocean. Robert Johnson told me an incident which occurred on a trip to India. He was walking through the city with a devout Hindu friend. They passed a beggar, and Robert gave him some money. The Hindu remonstrated with him and told him that he should not do that. Robert replied that he was doing it for himself and not for the beggar. Within that framework his action was considered permissible.

Death and war in these cultures are not seen as evils in the same way as they are where love is central. Death may be a blessing and release, and so life may seem much cheaper. In the opening passage of the *Bhagavad-gītā*, the human hero is talking with the god Krishna. He has mobilized his army against his foe, but he protests that he does not want to go into battle and kill all those people. Krishna reminds him that he should not have such compunctions, since these people are only illusion. This attitude is not perverse. It flows quite logically and necessarily from this religious and philosophical picture of the universe. Among those touched by this point of view there is little charity required of human beings except within the family group. The situation was similar to that among the Jews of Jesus' time to which Jesus addressed many of his stories about love.

Another Picture of Reality

There is another picture of reality which might even be called the natural one. Most human beings hold to it where they have not been influenced by one of the previous two. I shall present this picture in its most developed form as found in Jesus of Nazareth and the Early Church. Obviously it can be found in many stages of development.

The most important conviction which is expressed in the following diagram is that both physical and spiritual realms of existence are real and valuable. Indeed they are interrelated. Human beings share in both aspects of reality and indeed are often in tension between the two. Humans who are not relating to both aspects of experience are basically out of touch with reality. Therefore they are likely to be neurotic, psychotic or morally deficient.

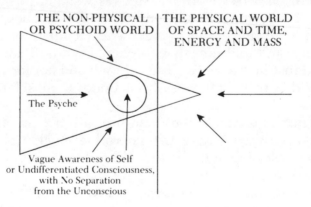

THE NON-PHYSICAL OR PSYCHOID WORLD

THE PHYSICAL WORLD OF SPACE AND TIME, ENERGY AND MASS

The Psyche

Vague Awareness of Self or Undifferentiated Consciousness, with No Separation from the Unconscious

There are creative and destructive elements of reality which operate within both aspects of experience, and they can influence human beings for good or evil. Within the individual there is the idiot and the murderer and also a capacity for sacrificial love. Human beings are in tension between the spiritual and physical worlds and between the

36

good and evil in both. Prayer and meditation can bring us into touch with the creative loving center of reality. This meditative experience, however, is not complete until we let this contact with Divine Love spill out through us to other human beings. There is no possible separation between genuine spirituality and its expression through acts of kindness and mercy, through social action and loving concern for *individuals.* The subject of the devotional life deals with coming to know the loving center of reality which Jesus portrayed and about which he told stories. Morality, ethics and Christian action are simply allowing that love to move out through us to other human beings in various circumstances.

Individual existence does not necessarily cease with death. Physical life and history usually provide the basis for the uniqueness of the ongoing development of human beings, but physical existence does not exhaust human existence. Human beings have an eternal destiny to be transformed more and more into the reality of the God of Love whom they worship.

Emotions like love and desire, if they are properly understood, can spur us forward on the spiritual journey. They are not to be eliminated, but purified. We need to bear the tension of that paradoxical state where we are both detached from inferior attachments and then attached to God in love and to human beings in concern and caring.

We human beings are more than our egos and our consciousness. We are more than our emotions and unconsciousness. Our task is to allow our total being to be transformed so that conscious and unconscious become one individuated whole. This usually takes longer than a human life. We may well need the eternity which most likely stretches out before us.

The creative center of reality is often described within this framework as Divine Love or the Divine Lover. This is true not only of mystical Christianity, but of Plato, Sufism and Hassidism. Love by its very nature is free gift and grace. We cannot earn it. We do not live loving lives primarily in order to get something for our action or to nudge ourselves toward perfection, but rather because loving is our deepest nature as revealed in the structure of the universe of which we are part. Most of the forward mutations in spiritual growth are given as we open ourselves to love within and without and allow that love to operate in us.

The question then arises: If indeed love and not hate or icy separation or indifference is the center of the universe, why is love so seldom observed in our world? Why is it that the law of the jungle, of power and strength and tooth and claw appears so often to be more central to our history and our human race than the practice of love?

The power struggle between Christian nations and the Arabs outpictures this ruthless struggle in devastating clarity. For nearly fourteen centuries this inhuman story of violence, intrigue, betrayal and arrogance has been acted out throughout the world. The Bantam/Britannica book, *The Arabs*, reveals a conflict in which love has been noticeable by its absence. In a ruthless, jungle-like world like ours we need something as startling and overpowering as a resurrection from a crucifixion to convince us that love is an essential constituent of this universe. Even with this belief most Christians have done little better than the Arabs. This brings us to the problem of evil.

The Problem of Evil

Christianity alone of the major religions of humankind deals head on with the problem of evil.[3] It does not offer a rational answer, but it does provide a practical solution. The message of Christianity is a story about God, about Love. He knew the misery of human beings and their disobedience and confusion. Unlike Luther who exclaimed that if he were the Lord God he would smash them to pieces, God continued to try to show human beings how far off the track they were. When they would not listen to the prophets, God came as a human being, a humble human being born in a stable within a stable-like world. Love took over the whole of the person of Jesus rather than just touching the outer periphery of the human psyche as in most human beings. Naturally Evil (Satan, the Devil, the old serpent, the rampaging lion) counterattacked. First of all he tried to sow doubt in Joseph's mind about the origin of this child. Then through Herod he tried to tidy things up and eliminate the child, followed by the flight to Egypt and exile there. When Jesus began his ministry in Nazareth, he was received with great acclaim, but Satan brought opposition first through the religious leaders of his people, then through the Roman government, and finally through the indifference of the populace. In the end the Evil One saw Love nailed to the cross, powerless, conquered; and the Evil One rubbed his hands in glee.

But Jesus did not remain dead. He rose again from the dead. The importance of this event is not that it gives us immortal life (I fear we have that whether we want it or not). The resurrection gives concrete historical evidence that Love is able to overcome the separation, hate and destructiveness pitted against us. It shows Love's ultimate relatedness to the center of reality. Thus we know that as we turn inward to this conquering Divine Lover, we turn to one who knows our misery and suffering, who has overcome the Evil One and who gives us the understanding and power to do the same. This does not depend upon our goodness or virtue. It is pure gift. Love is ultimately triumphant, and so are all of us when we allow Love to operate through our lives.

This story tells us a lot about the way God values human beings. God went to a lot of trouble and sacrifice to deliver human beings from the domination of and addiction to the influence of the Evil One. This redeeming action is performed for all human beings, and therefore all are valuable and unique. No individual is expendable. Those whom God died for, no human may use. Each person has a destiny and unique value to the Divine Lover. What I do unto the least of these, my brothers and sisters, I do unto God.

Just as I can turn inward and find the presence of God's Spirit within me, so as I learn truly to love other human beings I find the same Spirit within them. We can learn of God through our brothers and sisters when we meet them in love.

My meditative contact with the Divine Lover is completed only when some other human beings or group of

39

people feel more loved and cared for by me because of that contact. And conversely, no study of the physical realm is complete until it is related to the center of meaning and of love and is also related to the growth and welfare of human beings.

Eternal life is neither a matter of successive reincarnations nor absorption into Nirvana. It is rather the continuing development and growth of my capacity to love in the presence of others like me under the guidance of the Divine Lover. It is more like a joyous banquet than a void.

The relationship between teacher and student, master and learner, is not one of subservience, but rather of interchange and increasing trust and love and openness. There are no Christian gurus.

The potential for human growth and transformation is infinite. Sharing in the fullness of the sons and daughters of God is open to all. Growth goes on in the next world as well as this one, and we may even be able to change the direction of our life in the next life.

In the final analysis, growth and transformation are a gift, not the result of our own efforts. Childlike trust and loving faithfulness may be more important than wisdom, reason and strict discipline. The person who has had few opportunities to develop intellectually or socially may come to the same level of spiritual development as the one who is spiritually adept. We can look down on no one.

Christian religious practice which does not result in a horizontal outreach to suffering and lost human beings has gone astray. No Christian can have total peace while there is bloodshed, war, racial tension, discrimination, prejudice, poverty, overpopulation, human agony, or a foul prison system. There is often a tension between the sense of joy in the presence of the Divine Lover and living in the actual world so often devoid of his love.

It is difficult to treat human beings in this way. We seem to have a strong desire to ignore, to destroy, and to use other human beings. The murderer and idiot are within each of us. Evil touches us from within as well as from without.

This story about Jesus also tells a lot about the nature

40

of this evil in the universe. It is quite different from Persian dualism where good and evil are co-equal gods and are still fighting; the outcome of the conflict has not been decided. Indeed the resolution of the conflict in the Persian religion depends to a degree on what human beings do. Christianity is also quite different from the view of Gnosticism, which is a perversion of dualism. In this view evil is identified with matter and good is equated with spirituality. We shall say more about this point of view in a later chapter.

And where does this evil or Evil One come from? That is the sixty-four dollar question. There is another ancient Christian story which is based on the Book of Revelation (12:7) and tells of the revolt of the angels in heaven. One of the brightest and best of these angels, Lucifer, decided that heaven was not run efficiently enough, that love was not the way to operate the universe. He gathered a group of disgruntled angels and tried to take over heaven, but St. Michael threw Satan out of heaven. As tradition has it, he plummeted down to earth where he hit with so much force that he created a fiery cavern in the earth which was to be known as hell and pushed up a mountain opposite to hell known as Mount Purgatory. The devil himself, however, was frozen in a cake of ice in the center of the earth, the perfect symbol of the isolation of those who reject the way of love. Heaven continued much as it had always been, unchanged by the revolt. Earth, however, was overrun by the followers of Satan who came down with him. They cause much of the havoc among men and women. Jesus came to deliver humans from the power of the Evil One and his retainers.

Evil is then only a subsidiary, created power, which love does not utterly destroy simply because it is love. Those in touch with the living God in the end need not fear this evil. Evil is derivative, but at present it is very real, particularly for those who choose some other way than that of the God of love.[4]

One of the greatest of all Christian works of art is Dante's *Divine Comedy*. In incomparable poetry he describes his spiritual journey from the dark woods of his confusion through the depth of hell. Coming out of hell at the base of Mount Purgatory, he climbs it and passes through the ten spheres of heaven. At last, in the celestial white rose, the very dwelling of the triune Deity, he comes into the presence of God and here he finds the consummation of life's meaning which he describes in these final words of his poetic vision:

> Yet, as a wheel moves smoothly, free from jars,
> My will and my desire were turned by love,
> The love that moves the sun and the other stars.[5]

Very few people, including Christians, really believe that love describes the essential nature of God, the ultimate structure of the universe. Most of us fear rather than love God. We envision God as a despotic ruler before whom we must cringe or an irascible and undependable center of power. At best we picture him as a just judge (with very little mercy) before whom we come for judgment. Most of us who have much self-knowledge know that we have made a botch of our lives. So we come in fear and trembling and come as seldom as possible. This is tragic indeed, as it is very nearly impossible for Love to give its blessings to those who fear it. As a parent I know how difficult it is for me to express my love as long as my children fear me. And those who do not have the love of God and his mercy pouring into them find it very difficult, if not impossible, to give this kind of love to others.

It is strange that love is so seldom the central message of recent theology. This is difficult to understand when love is so central in the teaching and life of Jesus, so central to the Christian story and so central to the lives of the saints, those who have made the greatest impact on Christian history.

Perhaps we can only recognize the centrality of love as we have met Love and then allowed this love to pour through us. Much current theology is influenced by the introspections of two men who never had a mature love for anyone. Both Kierkegaard and Nietzsche were crippled in their capacity to love. Religious thinking which looks to these two for inspiration forgets how men and women are found of God, how they come to know and be known of him. The Christian God dies when we do not look for him in love. And rationalistic theology, Thomistic, existential or process, does not give love its central place. From this point of view we come to know God largely by rational reflection. There is little place for love in rational reflection. Love belongs to another kind of knowing quite different from reason, as the passage quoted from Jung reminds us.

Charles Williams is one of the few modern religious writers to write of the theological importance of love in *The Theology of Romantic Love.*

Those who love are those most likely to know Love and its eternal meaning and significance. Karl Jaspers states this in a little book to which he contributed, *Death to Life:* "The consciousness of immortality needs no knowledge, no guarantee, no threat. It lies in love, in this marvelous reality in which we are given to ourselves. We are mortal when we are without love and immortal when we love." And again, "I achieve immortality to the extent that I love.... I dissipate into nothingness as long as I live without love and therefore in chaos. As a lover I can see the immortality of those who are united to me in love."[6]

How Can We Love?

Growing in the capacity to love may begin in one of several ways. We may receive a direct experience of Divine Love or an intuition of its importance and may then try to live it out. Unless we have some others who agree with us, such a vision is very difficult to live, for it seems so at odds with what the world looks like. However, most of us get started as we get some glimmer of the beauty and power of Love through our church life and teaching, through Scripture, the Eucharist, or someone's loving action. Some of us may try to express that vision in action toward other people. Usually we find we cannot love and give up the task in disillusionment. Many social-action oriented ministers whom I have known have had this experience. They often end up as secular counselors. Or they decide that they had better find out if indeed there is a Divine Lover who can direct and empower them in their loving. Then they may begin to look around for ways of prayer and meditation which can bring them to that source of love and power that they need if they are going to be creative in their actions of caring and love. On the other hand, there are the introverts who read the Bible or perceive in the liturgy that there is love and mercy and forgiveness for all men and women who desire it. Then they begin to take prayer and meditation seriously and spend time with the Divine Lover. St. Teresa writes: "For mental prayer in my opinion is nothing else than an intimate sharing between friends: it means taking time frequently to be alone with Him who we know loves us."[7] They find, however, that as they meet Love, they are obliged to try to express love. This is as difficult for the introvert as stopping and turning inward is for the extrovert.

This process may be pictured in another diagram which shows two people facing each other within the space-time box. We begin on the path of loving as we realize that love is important and that it usually comes through the religious institution, represented by the church. Then eventually we turn inward and meet the source of love, and allow this love to flow into us and help us love ourselves. Thus we can open ourselves up in actions of love so that this love may flow out toward other human beings. Christian love, perhaps all genuine loving, is not so much what we feel and do, as what we allow Love to do through us.

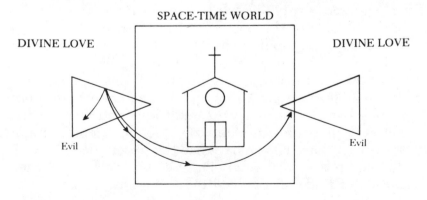

SPACE-TIME WORLD

DIVINE LOVE

DIVINE LOVE

Evil

Evil

Love is the only reality which consistently is able to open the citadel of other human beings to us, and often this takes years of continued patient caring. It is frightening to open ourselves to another being or to God. We become vulnerable. As others open themselves to us, Love and love begin to flow out through them. It is nearly impossible to allow ourselves to be truly loved without loving in response. Then it appears as if the Divine Lover were communicating with himself, using two of us human beings as the occasion and lifting us up into his love at the same time.

The following pages are attempts to describe the methods, practices, attitudes and actions by which we may begin to open ourselves up to other human beings. This presupposes that we can know the loving God. Coming to know the Divine Lover is the subject of another book of mine, *The Other Side of Silence: A Guide to Christian Meditation,*[8] and so we shall say a little about the practice of prayer.

First of all we shall deal with the necessary first step, the fine art of loving ourselves. We shall then examine the nature and practice of listening without which love is impossible. There are certain practices and attitudes which facilitate love within the family and among those in other intimate relationships. This leads quite naturally to the subject of sexuality, marriage and love. Then we shall study the nature of the human personality so that we may know better how to love human beings who differ as much as we do from one another. The subject of hostility and possessiveness, two zeros of love, will demand our subsequent attention. We shall then look at ways in which we can love the acquaintance, the person with whom one has close but not intimate contact. After that we shall take up Jesus' most difficult commandment that we love our enemies. Sometimes the stranger is treated even more destructively than the enemy, and we shall see how we can express love to the stranger. This leads into the subject of love and social action. We shall conclude with a brief discussion of the incredible results which love accomplishes in human life.

4

The Fine Art
of Loving Ourselves

Much conventional and popular Christianity gives the impression that it is wrong to love ourselves. Instead we are supposed to do away with our concern for ourselves, get rid of ego, smash the "self" and be concerned only for others. The attitude of much Jansenism (at one time so prevalent in religious orders) and Puritanism (often a characteristic of Protestantism in the recent past) is that we are really nasty, ugly, despicable creatures who need to be kept under tight control so that we are not carried off to hell. Calvin himself wrote that self-love is a "pest."[1] Christian education began in the United States only when the Puritan notion that children were little monsters was abandoned. From this former point of view education, and Christian education in particular, was a process of taming the monster in children and adults. The work of Horace Bushnell in the middle of the nineteenth century brought about a new understanding of human nature and education.

How we view the nature of human beings will determine to a large extent the way we treat human beings. If we view human beings as nothing but a complex pattern of conditioned responses, then we will select some goal and try to shape them toward this. May heaven have mercy on us if we are being shaped toward that goal by people who are criminals by profession. Some recognized governments are little better than this. If we see children as little monsters, we try to tame the nasty beasts. If we see them as only conscious, rational beings, we will naturally try to fill them with the right ideas. There is nothing more to education than this. If we take seriously the picture of the human being which we presented in the last chapter, then our task is quite different. Our task is to enable children to know they are cared for by us and by God. Our task is also to enable others and *ourselves* to come to wholeness and to grow to our full potential.

This wholeness is difficult to describe. There are many parts of me which need to function together. I am not just rationality and consciousness or just feelings or only conditioned responses or only pure spirit. I am all of these to some degree. These various parts of me need to work together as an harmonious whole. Some of the depth of me is bright and beautiful and loving, and some of me is dark, questionable, destructive, and dangerous. My task is to redeem what is redeemable within the darkness and bring the whole of my being into one entire, integral human center of action and of feeling and of being. Wholeness means to function as a unit rather than allowing the various parts of me to take control of me and act autonomously.

This is what Jesus meant when he said that we should have a single eye. We are not to have a double eye or triple eye, but a single one, a single point of reference from which we operate. If I do not try to have a single eye, a single unitary wholeness, then anything is likely to pop out of me at any time and I am not responsible. As Meyeroff points out so clearly, there is no consistent love where there is no responsibility.

Again we can see from the last diagram in Chapter 3 that we cannot come to the full potential of which we are capable until we love. And this is not possible by our own action alone, but it can happen as we allow Divine Love to

47

move in and through us and transform us into our unbeliev-able potential as daughters and sons of God. And all along we thought we were only waifs and bastards. Loving other human beings means trying to create conditions by which they reach their potential as human beings. Loving our-selves has the same meaning.

We are so apt to confuse self-love, genuine caring for ourselves, with selfishness and egotism. They are very, very different. Meyeroff describes egocentricity as morbid pre-occupation with ourselves and opaqueness to the needs of others. Fromm points out that the selfish people are inter-ested only in themselves, want inner and outer things only for themselves. They find no pleasure in the joy and growth of others, or in giving, but only in receiving. He goes on to point out that selfishness and self-love, far from being of the same class or category, are actually opposite. Truly selfish people not only have difficulty in loving others, but they seldom love themselves either.

Fromm points out Meister Eckhart's exquisite state-ment about self-love: "If you love yourself, you love every-body else as you do yourself. As long as you love another person less than you love yourself, you will not really suc-ceed in loving yourself; but if you love all alike, including yourself, you will love them as one person and that person is both God and man. Thus he is a great and righteous per-son who, loving himself, loves all others equally."[2] Often the people who appear unselfish or make a fetish of being unselfish are trying to tie others to them for future gain. Parents often do this to their children. In other people un-selfishness is simply the inability to say "no" to any de-mand. They do not value themselves enough to see that they have their own requirements for growth and that do-ing what others want is not unselfishness at all.

A woman came to me for counseling who was being driven ragged by family and friends. She was very capable, but she could not say "no" to anyone. Someone had given me a ceramic figure. It had a depressed and dejected ex-pression and had footprints all over it. I gave it to her and she kept it by the telephone to remind her that it was im-moral for her to always say "yes" to every request. Being unselfish does not mean letting the world walk all over us. There is a lovely story about Dr. Jung dealing with this very problem. He told one of his patients who wanted an appointment that he had no more available time during a specific week. During that week this patient was sailing on the Lake of Zurich and saw Jung sitting on the wall at the back of his home, with his bare feet dangling in the water. At the next visit with Jung the patient was very angry, complaining that he had lied. He replied, "No, I had an appointment with myself, one of the most important ones I ever have."

As we begin to love ourselves and value what we are in spite of our ugliness and stupidity, then we are free to like other people and treat them with loving concern. Once we have come to have a genuine regard for ourselves, then we don't always have to be on the defensive by drawing attention to the faults of others. We don't have to protect our egos with a shield of critical gossip or anger. We need no longer be worried about how others may be talking about us; we know how we stand with ourselves and that we are trying to do our best. What others say won't add to or subtract from that assessment or throw us. We won't be hurt over slights or injuries because we know that the other people probably didn't mean them—and even if they did, it was a piece of poor judgment on their part.

We have the inside story on ourselves. If we can lovingly accept what we are and what we are trying to become, we can see that the negative opinions of others are simply poor taste on their part. The uninformed opinions of other people no longer bother us. And then a wonderful thing begins to happen. We can begin to forget about ourselves and turn out to other people and think about them and what concerns them and how they react and how we can show them love.

St. Catherine of Siena likewise believed that there could be no fire of deep loving without the wood of self-knowledge. To her friend and confessor, Raymond of Capua, she wrote: "I would have you never cease increasing the fuel for the fire of holy desire, that is, the wood of self-knowledge. This is the wood that nourishes and feeds the fire of divine love; this love is acquired by the knowledge of self and of the inestimable love of God. . . . The more fuel one gives to the fire, so much the more increases the warmth of love of Christ and of neighbor. So remain hidden in the knowledge of self."[3]

In Leviticus the Hebrews are commanded: "You shall love your neighbor as yourself" (Lev. 19:18). Jesus pointed to this passage as half of the summary of the law. The obvious implication, which has been pointed out by many writers, is that we cannot very well love our neighbors unless we do love ourselves.

What It Means To Love Myself

If I am to love myself, I need first of all to know what I am truly like. So many of us today get caught up in drugs or alcohol or in some form of busyness simply because we cannot bear to turn inward and quietly look at all of ourselves. We shall say more about how difficult this is later on. As the Arthur Miller story reminds us, we all have within us a part of us which seems like pure idiot. This is the part that never does the right thing, always seems to put its foot in its mouth, falls on its face, forgets appointments, lets others down, can't remember birthdays and gets sexually aroused at the most inappropriate times. And then there is the murderer within, often called the Hitler within. It screams for blood and destruction and is bent on violence and hatred even when there is no reason for it. Those who believe in the total depravity of human beings subscribe to the idea that there is nothing in us but murderer and idiot. There is good reason to avoid looking at ourselves and trampling ourselves underfoot if this is our view of human beings.

There is also a genuine caring side of us which wishes to give warmth and love. It is genuinely interested in other people and even in itself. It is the very spirit of Love within us. It is most naturally in the love of a mother for a small child, of a lover for the beloved, or among genuine friends. A strange fire is lighted and burns within us when we love in this way.

To truly love, I need to look at all of me, including the

50

light and the dark. Then I can control the negative and destructive parts of myself without giving way to despair. The people who think of themselves as most guileless and harmless or most dangerous (seeing only one side of themselves) often create the worst havoc.

How do I come to know all of myself? I have discussed this in *The Other Side of Silence*, where I emphasize the fact that it is impossible to pray and meditate effectively unless we bring all of ourselves before God. Likewise we cannot love ourselves unless we know what is there within us to love and realize how difficult it is to love that inner zoo.

First of all we need to stop and listen to the depth of ourselves. This is very difficult without times of silence and aloneness. For many people a journal has been a tremendous aid in this process of reflection and self-knowledge. Listening to my dreams can also help by revealing what is going on in me when my conscious control is removed. Dreams, particularly fearful and nightmarish ones, often tell me what I have refused to look at and consider. Examining my experiences of fear and anger and depression often gives me clues about submerged parts of my multifaceted self. My loves and hates tell me more about me than about the people toward whom they are directed. My fantasy and daydreams, the stories I dream up and the fairy tales I enjoy all tell me about the monsters, angels and fairies which populate my soul. Often, however, I cannot bear all of this self-knowledge unless I have a friend, a companion, a spiritual guide, a listener who gives me objectivity and encouragement as well as reaction and response.

As I begin to see what is within me, then it is my task to take responsibility for what is there. I need to take charge of my life. I have a certain amount of freedom and I can develop a consistent pattern of action by picking a goal and working to make it the central direction of my life. I need to choose among the elements which I find within me and decide which of them I wish to express and which I do not want to express. *This is, perhaps, the first step toward becoming a loving person.*

There are some religious enthusiasts who believe that

51

all they need to do is to turn their lives over to the Spirit. According to them, the Spirit will do all that is necessary, and they have no responsibility for good or evil. This is pure nonsense. The God of Love does not possess our lives and run them for us. Only the Evil One and his minions are set on doing that (and the devil need not make me do it). The Divine Lover can seldom if ever navigate the ships of our lives unless we have first of all learned some navigational skill and assist him. Weakly developed motivation produces the same effect as a fragmented psyche. When the personality is weak we need to develop discipline and courage to take responsibility for our lives. God can seldom do much with a life where we are not putting our best into making our lives work. Weakness and lack of discipline may be greater deterrents to the coming of the Kingdom among human beings than actual evil and maliciousness. M. Scott Peck points out that genuine love is impossible without first developing discipline.

Once I know who I am and gather my will together so that I can act in a unified way, then it is my task to find a goal toward which I can direct my life. When we do not have some conscious goal, we are usually run by an unconscious one. For over fifty years I have been mulling over possible goals for my life, and the only one which satisfies the deepest strivings of my soul and the questing reach of my mind is the one I have stated earlier: To know the love of God expressed in Jesus Christ and to share that love with all those around me.

As I really try to take charge of myself I realize that I do not and apparently cannot achieve this kind of goal by myself. One of the most discouraging things on the pathway toward Christian wholeness and love is that the harder we try, the less headway we sometimes seem to make. We find that we are not able to shape our lives in the pattern that we desire. There are negative and destructive forces within us which we cannot control. Paul cries out in Romans 7: "I do not do the good I want to do; instead I do the evil that I don't want to do." This seems to be our human plight and we realize that in order to do better we have a need for other struggling human beings and for God as our personal friend and companion.

The church is meant to be a fellowship of those who know the filth of their own feet and are willing to wash the feet of others and allow their own feet to be washed by others. As I have said elsewhere, the church is not a museum for saints, but a hospital for sinners. When the church is really the church, it is a place where we can go in our discouragement about ourselves and find other unjudging people who have found some answers, methods and ways of doing better. From personal experience and from observation I *know* that we human beings seldom go far on the way toward Christian fulfillment unless we have others who understand and are willing to bear with us. One of the most important things for those who would grow in love of themselves is to find a fellowship of caring people with whom to relate. Some of us need spiritual friends with whom we can discuss all aspects of our lives. The capacity to love others seldom, if ever, grows in a vacuum.

And then there is a need for a relationship with the Divine Lover himself. I doubt if I could continue long to try to love myself, if I were not aware that there is a being of light and love to whom I can turn and where I am always received with understanding, without judgment, with concern and love. When I realize that there is such a "being of light" (as he is called by many of the people interviewed in *Life after Life* by Raymond Moody), then I realize something else just as important. I realize that when I do not love myself I may be rejecting the love of God, saying that I know better than the Divine Lover, that I am not lovable or capable of being loved. The essential quality of the Evil One is that he thought he knew better than God his nature and the nature of reality. When I refuse the love of God by thinking myself unworthy or incapable of being loved, I step in the company of his Infernal Majesty. Ultimately I find myself valuable when I find that God not only tolerates me, but seeks my company no matter what I am or have been or have done, and knowing full well what I might become and what I might do.

Then I need others who have shared in this experience who can confirm and support me with fellowship and understanding. None but the most heroic can survive with only divine love. We are human beings and we need to give and receive human love as well as love from God if we are to survive and grow. In order to truly love myself, I find that I must be honest with myself and try to bring all aspects of my complex inner being into one focus. I am half beast and half angel. Sometimes that beast is a purring kitten and sometimes a charging water buffalo. Likewise the angelic part of me may be urging me toward sacrificial love or toward pride and scorn. My task is to bring the beast and the angel together in perfect harmony. To accomplish this task I see then my need to expose myself to those human and spiritual influences which can facilitate this harmony.

Mary Stewart has written three moving novels about Merlin and King Arthur. In *The Crystal Cave, The Hollow Hills,* and *The Last Enchantment,* the hero believes that he is a rejected, bastard child only to discover that he is really the king's accepted and cherished son. The process of Christian self-realization is something like this. We come to know that we are more than we dreamed we could be, and with this realization, this experience of acceptance, we are flooded with power to undertake our new destiny.

The Dangers of Self-Rejection and Self-Denial

Those people who refuse to look deep within themselves and take loving responsibility for what they discover can fall into serious moral, psychological and physical problems. Great havoc is let loose upon society by people with good intentions who are unaware of their own idiocy and murderous hostility. The refusal to love ourselves can result in four different catastrophes.

In the first place, I may *project* the dark destructiveness (the murderer within) out upon other human beings. When I refuse to look at my inner idiot and murderer I am likely to see him in my stepmother, my brother, the people next door, a different race, a different religious group, a different political party or the nation with whom we are at

54

war. In short, I see him in any person or group that I do not know or understand. This mechanism is evident in racial and class tension, in most fears we have of others, in most social chaos. Paracelsus, the great medieval physician, reminds us that the more we understand, the more likely we are to love, notice and see. The greater the knowledge of ourselves and others, the greater our love is likely to be. When we project we cut off this avenue toward love by seeing our own evil in another and refusing to face it in ourselves. Projection is one of the Evil One's most effective techniques. Genuine self-knowledge and love robs the destructive forces in the universe of one of their cruelest weapons. When you can't stand hypocrites, look within; you are probably projecting your own hypocrisy!

Whenever I have strong emotional reactions toward another person with no particularly good reason, I can suspect projection at work. When I was a young man I could not abide one specific political leader, Franklin Delano Roosevelt. As I began to know more of myself I found that the very quality which I disliked most in him, his use of every means to achieve his ends, was one of my own qualities which I could not abide and would not face.

This inner destructiveness can also be turned upon ourselves. In Freud's later writings he wrote of a death wish which operates within the human psyche and seeks to suck us back into the state of non-living matter, into inorganicity, into death. He saw war as the outward projection of this death wish. When these destructive tendencies are *introjected*, turned in upon ourselves, a host of other problems appear. The classical, devasting study of this process is Karl Menninger's *Man Against Himself.* My students at Notre Dame found this book frightening. It stripped away their defenses and showed them how much of their sickness, neurosis and antisocial behavior was the result of refusal to face their own inner death wish. According to Menninger (and my own counseling has confirmed what he has written), everything from neurosis and psychosis to alcoholism and multiple surgery, self-mutilation and a lot of our physical sickness can be laid at the door of the destructive tendencies within us which we resolutely refuse to look at or deal with. They take their toll on our minds, bodies and loved ones.

When I was studying in Zurich, Switzerland, I was trying to get at the roots of myself as well as to learn about how the human psyche operates. Indeed I have found that trying to study human beings without knowing ourselves can lead into frustration and folly. I was talking with a friend one day and complaining about a disordered digestive system. She asked me what had caused it. I told her my story of going on a trip and not taking the time for a decent meal. Instead I had picked up a loaf of bread and some sausage and gone off on my trip. The friend asked why I hadn't taken time for a good meal and I replied that I couldn't afford the cost. She replied very frankly, "That's nonsense. Look at the amount you have spent to study here for these months; a few dollars more would have made no difference. You were unconsciously flailing yourself." I realized that she was right. The next time I took a trip I passed through Feldkirch, Austria. Quite consciously I sought out the best restaurant in town, *Der Löwen,* and had my first cordon bleu. This was a sacramental action of self-love, one I will never forget. I had not realized until that time how much of my self-denial was predicated not on virtue, but on self-rejection.

A few people now and then allow this destructive aspect of their personality to rise up out of the depth of them and take over their entire personalities; they become instruments of evil. Few people have the discipline of Hitler or Genghis Khan or Charles Manson. These people made the service of destructive power an aim in itself. Erich Fromm has written an interesting study of Hitler's destructiveness in his book, *The Anatomy of Human Destructiveness.* Charles Williams describes a person being possessed by evil in his novel *Shadows of Ecstasy.*

Most of us do not allow our aggressive violence to take possession of us. It emerges now and then in fits of anger and hatred, but seldom does it take over as in those instances where the admired and accepted Boy Scout leader, church member, or good neighbor suddenly goes berserk and becomes a killer. One of the dangers of war is that it not only allows but encourages the killer in us to take over. It is difficult to put our murderer back to bed when we come back to more "normal" times. Many primitive people live constantly in this state, and the endemic war they wage against their neighbors seems to drain off this destructiveness. If we do not know our capability for violence and destructiveness, we are in no position to handle it when it does emerge out of the depth of the unconscious maelstrom.

The most dangerous way in which these destructive urges appear is in ambivalence. We are committed to neither good nor evil. We are neither hot nor cold. We express our violence and anger when we feel them and our love and concern and tenderness when we feel like doing that also. In the current honesty fetish, expressing what we feel at the moment is almost seen as virtuous. However few things are more destructive to human relations and genuine communication and caring than thoughtless honesty. One never knows what to expect. There is no real person to relate to.

In counseling with young people I have discovered that this kind of ambivalence on the part of parents toward their children is responsible for more confusion and neurotic despair than any other form of behavior. If parents are consistently angry or hostile or cruel or kind or indifferent, children can adjust to these attitudes. When, however, those responsible for children have no consistent mode of behavior, they often create chaos. Pavlov demonstrated that dogs can be driven mad with ambivalence. Modern brainwashing procedures are systematized ambivalence. If we wish to really louse up children, we treat them well and kindly when we feel warm and use them as whipping posts when our ugliness and nastiness emerge. There is no better way to destroy people. To give love only when we feel that people deserve it is not loving other people but using them, destroying them.

How many well-intentioned parents fail at this point and betray a tragic unpredictable ambivalence! In their very attempt at discipline, they destroy. Whenever withdrawal of warmth and love is used as a method of trying to direct or control children or those dependent upon us, they are likely to feel that they have no value in themselves, in their own being, but only in their actions. How difficult it is for us ever to come to a genuine self-love until some others have treated us with love whether we were good or bad!

Most often we are treated ambivalently by others because they have never received genuine love from anyone themselves, and so the dark strain passes from generation to generation. Van der Post writes: "There are no panderers, procurers and pimps so cunning and irresistible as those parents who themselves have not experienced love."[4] They simply do not know how not to be ambivalent, and they leave their children in shambles. Let me repeat: it is very difficult to love ourselves until we have been loved unconditionally by someone.

Six Practical Suggestions on Learning How To Love Ourselves

The first step toward self-love is a simple one. We need to make a conscious decision to see ourselves through the eyes of the Divine Lover. It is at this point that it is very helpful to start keeping a journal if one has not already done so before. It is very difficult to reflect in depth and to keep from going over the same ground again and again unless we keep some record of our intentions and progress toward genuine self-love. We may also have to reassess our value system and see why the idea of loving ourselves is so difficult for us to accept.

Some years ago I was meeting with a group of people who were considered authorities on the spiritual life. Instead of being stimulated by the experience, I found myself getting depressed because I didn't feel that these other people were listening to me. When I went up to my room to chew my psychic cud and take a good look at myself, I took up my journal and began to write. I then realized that I was beset with all sorts of negative feelings. First of all my pride was hurt; I wasn't appreciated. In other words I was afraid, and because I was afraid I was angry and I wanted

58

to put the others down. Secondly I was depressed. I wondered if I really did have anything to say, if I had any value. I realized that this attitude was close to egotism. I'd show them that I had something to say! How often I find that egotism covers up depression and meaninglessness. And then I realized that there was some solid, earthy lust bubbling away in me. As I got this all out there on paper I could laugh at myself and bring the whole sorry mess to the Christ who knew about me all the time and loved me just the same. I was then free to go back and feel and act like a human being.

The second step in loving myself is recognizing that everyone has a hard time doing so. I am not unique in this and I try not to get discouraged by what I find within me. Discouragement is very often only disillusioned egotism. One of the most penetrating statements of the difficulty most of us have loving ourselves was written by Dr. C. G. Jung. In his book, *Modern Man in Search of a Soul,* he states that it is impossible to touch the lives of other people in a creative way unless we love ourselves. We cannot accompany others a step on the way unless we accept the others without judgment or condemnation. Jung calls this behavior "unprejudiced objectivity." I would call it love. An attitude of judgment or condemnation toward ourselves will be picked up by other people whether we express it or not. He writes, "We cannot change anything unless we accept it. Condemnation does not liberate, it oppresses. I am the oppressor of the person I condemn, not his friend and fellow sufferer." He goes on to say that it is impossible not to condemn and judge unless we see and accept ourselves as we are. He then writes these words:

> Perhaps this sounds very simple, but simple things are always the most difficult. In actual life it requires the greatest discipline to be simple, and the acceptance of oneself is the essence of the moral problem and the epitome of a whole outlook upon life. That I feed the hungry, that I forgive an insult, that I love my enemy in the name of Christ— all these are undoubtedly great virtues. What I do

unto the least of my brethren, that I do unto Christ. But what if I should discover that the least amongst them all, the poorest of all the beggars, the most impudent of all the offenders, the very enemy himself—that these are within me, and that I myself stand in need of the alms of my own kindness—that I myself am the enemy who must be loved—what then? As a rule, the Christian's attitude is then reversed; there is no longer any question of love or long-suffering; we say to the brother within us "Raca," and condemn and rage against ourselves. We hide it from the world; we refuse to admit ever having met this least among the lowly in ourselves. Had it been God himself who drew near to us in this despicable form, we should have denied him a thousand times before a single cock had crowed.

The man who uses modern psychology to look behind the scenes not only of his patients' lives but more especially of his own—and the modern psychotherapist must do this if he is not to be merely an unconscious fraud—will admit that to accept himself in all his wretchedness is the hardest of tasks, and one which it is almost impossible to fulfill. The very thought can make us livid with fear. We therefore do not hesitate, but lightheartedly choose the complicated course of remaining in ignorance about ourselves while busying ourselves with other people and their troubles and sins. This activity lends us an air of virtue, and we thus deceive ourselves and those around us. In this way, thank God, we can escape from ourselves. There are countless people who can do this with impunity, but not everyone can, and these few break down on the road to Damascus and succumb to a neurosis. How can I help these persons if I am myself a fugitive, and perhaps also suffer from the *morbus sacer* [holy illness] of a neurosis? Only he who has fully accepted himself has "unprejudiced objectivity." But no one is justified in boasting that he has fully accepted himself. We can point to Christ, who offered his traditional bias as a sacrifice to the god in himself, and so lived his life as it was to the bitter end without regard for conventions or for the moral standards of the Pharisees.[5]

Sometimes we get so caught up in our ugliness that we forget that we have any virtues or value. This is no more honest than the refusal to face our darkness. We need to admit our worth and pay attention to our virtues. We fail to see what gifts and graces we have been given if we don't. An excellent exercise in self-love is to take an hour and sit down with our journal and write down in black and white all the good things about ourselves. We are intelligent, fairly good-looking, gracious, have a good singing voice, are good with feeble-minded children, find it easy to be still, have a good imagination, a strong will, a capacity for play, beautiful hair ... The list is endless. Without a concrete, conscious exercise of this kind, we seldom move toward mature self-love.

It is just as morally wrong to dislike, despise and devalue ourselves as it is to have these attitudes toward others. Perhaps it is worse, since it is refusal to accept God's love for us. Let us put it imaginatively. We are like silly, self-depreciating children cooped up in one tiny miserable cell of a great mansion. We have not thought ourselves good enough to live in the mansion, so we call to God to help us out of our mean, little cell or soul room. He comes and says to us, "Come out of this little cell and inherit the whole mansion. You are living in a cellar dungeon and the whole place is yours." But we look up and cry out, "Ah, Lord, but we are not worthy!" And then the Lord may become quite annoyed and may even say, "How dare you call unworthy the one for whom I died, the one to whom I come whenever I am called. You need to abandon this silly attitude in order to inherit the kingdom prepared for you from the foundation of the world. Of course you can creep back into your cell by yourself and stay there. But I know what is worthy. I came among men and women as a human being. I died for you. I come now when anyone desires me.

Put aside the pride of unworthiness and inherit what I have won for you."

If we do not try to value ourselves as Christ did, if we persist in hating ourselves, we are politely telling God that he didn't know what he was doing in sending his Son to us. We know better than he! The mystery of our faith, the mystery of Christian experience is this: God loves us and Jesus Christ would have died on the cross for us *even if we had been the only one!* Why he cares so much I can't imagine, but *I know* that this is the way God values us. How dare we then hate or mock these very selves whom God so greatly values! I know of no other religion which gives human beings such infinite worth.

The next step in loving ourselves is learning *to accept forgiveness from others.* It is far easier to forgive than to be forgiven. It is easier to give pardon than to accept it. Jesus is specific in telling us the importance of accepting forgiveness. He told his disciples that when they were bringing gifts to the altar and there remembered that their neighbor had anything against them, they were to leave the gift and go to be reconciled with their neighbor. Jesus did not say, "If you have something against your neighbor, go and forgive him," but "If your neighbor has something against you. . . ." In other words, if we have done something to our neighbor for which we have not tried to receive forgiveness, or for which we have not accepted forgiveness, then we are to leave our gifts before the altar and go to seek forgiveness.

A close friend of mine once offended me greatly. I was deeply hurt, but I cared for this friend, and so I forgave him. Even so, something happened to our friendship. We drifted apart. One day as we were talking I realized he couldn't accept my forgiveness and so he had felt unworthy of my friendship and had withdrawn from the relationship. We talked about it and he accepted my forgiveness, and we were reconciled. Through accepting my forgiveness he began to value himself.

In order to accept forgiveness, we need to value ourselves. In accepting forgiveness we come to an enhanced self-value. The Christian church is built on those who accepted forgiveness and loved God the more for it. Peter denied Jesus; John fled from him. Paul persecuted the risen Christ and tried to destroy his church. All accepted the forgiveness of God and became the founders of the church.

We need to take a chance and relate to other human beings as Jesus did, even if they betray us. We need to accept love even if it makes us vulnerable. We cannot love ourselves unless we let others love us. Nothing is sadder than the person who is loved and cannot feel it.

Seldom can we come to love ourselves except in this kind of interaction with others, accepting and being accepted, forgiving and being forgiven, loving and being loved. Few people can sit at home withdrawn and come to self-acceptance. It is something that is given in living fellowship with human beings. Seldom can we stay apart from others and come to love or value ourselves. No human being is an island. If we try to be one, we usually become less than fully human. As we live our lives openly and fully with other people, as we are accepted and accept each other—in spite of betrayal and hurt and being let down—then we manifest real courage and we grow in an appreciation, an acceptance and a love for ourselves.

The essence of the healing encounter between psychological counselors and counselees, between therapists and patients, consists of warm accepting concern. The counselees are accepted as they are and so they begin to accept themselves. Ideally this is what the church is for. It is supposed to be a fellowship filled with the compassion, the understanding and the love of Christ. If it were really such an accepting fellowship (rather than the handful of isolated individuals who happen to come together on a Sunday morning), then miracles of transformation would happen; we would find far less need for psychologists. But until that time comes, we must often find this part of our religion in a counseling situation.

The next step in trying to come to self-acceptance is an aspect of being honest with ourselves. In counseling with people from adolescence on I have discovered that most people feel guilty for the wrong things. They are judging themselves for the wrong mistakes, attitudes and vices. Often sexual peccadilloes are considered far worse than the more serious sins of pride and arrogance. Until I can look at myself with objectivity, it is nearly impossible for me to see what is good and what needs changing in my life. There is no point forgiving ourselves for actions for which we don't need forgiveness. We need to distinguish between our hangups and our sins.

Our task in loving ourselves is to be able to look deep and hard at what appears to be our disgusting ugliness. Then we can see that certain aspects of us are earthy and not evil; we are of the earth, earthy. There are certain attitudes which are ugly that we can change and that we need to work on. And then there is the dark hand of the inner murderer within who can only be changed as we forgive him as we do the inner idiot.

When I come to this point I find that I need some help beyond myself. I am at the end of my rope. It is then that the only help I know is to bring my psyche, deeply stained with destructiveness, before the Divine Lover. I have found that imaginative turning inward in meditative prayer is one of the best ways of coming to myself and accepting myself. I have used this basic image hundreds of times in many different ways.

I realize finally that there is no more help outside of me for my broken and hurting soul, and so I drag myself back into my own little soul room, out of the busy streets, and out of my confusions and angers and hurts. As I come into my soul room I am shocked to find the state of things— the tables are overturned, the dishes are stacked high in the kitchen, stinking refuse fills one corner. As I sit down and try to be quiet, a little voice perched on my left shoulder whispers: "You're no good. You never were any good. You will never be any good. Why don't you just give up, curse God and die?"

I think to myself. "This is an ugly mess. No wonder I don't come home to myself more often. Whenever I stop and am still, I have to come into this stable." Everytime I look for meaning and hope within, that little voice on my shoulder whispers: "There isn't any meaning; there isn't any hope; the idea that Christ rose from the dead is fiction. There is no hope for you. Why not sit down and rot?"

Then I have to summon up my courage, reject the subtle seductiveness of that voice, and say with strength: "I know that you are a deceiving, lying voice, a destructive spirit. I have known meaning and hope. Be still. You are a liar." As I then drift into true quietness I hear a soft, persistent knocking. It comes from the other side of my soul. The negative voice whispers once again that I should pay no attention to that knocking. It is illusion. Then I realize that the spirit which is speaking through that voice is afraid that I'll find some meaning and it will lose its power.

I go over to the other side of the room. There is a doorway. The knocking comes from the other side of a nearly forgotten door. I gather up my courage and ask the knocker to open the door and come in. I hear a voice which tells me that he cannot, for the door is bolted and the latch string is on my side. And so I open the door, and there stands the Lord of Life, the Light of the World, one hand with the print of a nail raised to knock, the other carrying a lantern. On his head is a crown of thorns which he carries almost with a touch of jest. He has overcome those who have tried to do him in.

For a while I can say nothing, and then I speak: "Lord, why are you here? What do you want of me? Certainly you don't want to come into my lousy soul room, inhabited by doubts and fears, destructive voices!" The Lord speaks to me in comfortable words: "Child, don't be silly. It is just because you are attacked that I come. I know that you can't possibly handle these dark forces by yourself and that you need me, and I come to let you share in the victory. I have conquered them."

I cannot understand and say to him: "Why me? Why do you bother to come to me?" He replies that he loves me and that it is his very nature to love, and that he will come to anyone who listens to the knock and opens the door, and that he will come into that soul and loosen the hold of the darkness and give new courage and strength.

I welcome the Lord into my soul room. He embraces

me and sets the table on its feet. He gets bread and wine and makes Eucharist. Then we laugh and talk, and he tells me that he is with me until the end of the world and that I am to go out and treat others as he is treating me. Then I look at my soul room and it has been transformed, renewed. As the Lord leaves he turns and says to me, "Thank you for letting me come into your life and give you meaning and value. I am with you here whenever you wish me. Love yourself and others who need your love, as I have loved you."

When I finish such a time of prayer I find it easier to love myself. I usually have a new sense of peace and a new desire to go out to other human beings.

5

Love and Listening

It is impossible for us to love other people unless we listen to them. We simply cannot love without learning to listen. The kind of listening I am talking about is listening which does not judge or evaluate. It is open and objective, and we shall describe it in greater detail later in this chapter.

These words about listening may seem radical inasmuch as there has been so little emphasis on listening within the Christian community. Often among some enthusiastic Christians there is no attempt to find out where I am and gently lead me to the loving Christ. Instead I often discover a steamroller intensity which only desires that I agree or submit to their point of view. Evangelism which is not characterized by love and attentive listening is just not Christian.

Why is listening so important to love? The answer is quite simple. Each and every person is unique. There are different types of people and they have different value systems. We have been shaped by very different positive and negative circumstances. Just as no two leaves upon any tree are *exactly* the same, so no two human beings are formed in exactly the same mold. We shall go further into these differences in a later chapter.

Genuine love is always centered in the need of the other person and in ministering to that need. Loving means giving others the concern, appreciation and understanding that they need. It is not a matter of giving what we feel like giving, but giving what the other needs for his or her present joy and future development. How can I possibly give that kind of concern and care and understanding unless I know the other human beings? How can I know others unless they disclose, reveal or unveil themselves to me? And how is this possible unless I listen to them? When we try to love without first knowing the needs of those around us, we are likely to be ministering to our own needs and not to theirs. We are probably projecting upon others.

One of the basic problems between spouses and between children and parents is that those on the giving end offer only what they want to give, what they feel like giving, without first discovering what the others want and need. To give without first finding out about other people is not love but rather a kind of selfishness. Real love goes out to others as they are, not as we think they are or as we want them to be. This requires that we listen. Listening is necessary within families and among friends. This is also true for teachers, doctors, clergy, social workers and even psychologists who fail to touch the lives of other people when they have not learned to listen.

Not only is each one of us unique, each one of us is also an impregnable fortress. As a rule, we only let others into the inner secret sanctuary of our soul as they knock with listening concern. First of all we let such persons into the outer courtyard, then into the castle itself; then step by step we lead them through the labryinthian passages of our inner being before we allow them to enter the very depth of ourselves, our shabby soul room.

One of the tragedies of powerful, superior, charismatic people is that they seldom really know and love other people. Often they force submission or possess others through a kind of mass hypnotism as Jim Jones did in Guyana. They do not meet the other in free interchange and love. Many years ago my wife and I took a teenager into our home. His family had thrown him out, and he had confided to me all his troubles, his fears, his deepest thoughts. The moment that he crossed the threshold of our home, however, I became an authority figure, a parent, and he was no longer able to share with me. I had not changed, but he saw me as a person with power over his life and I was no longer accepted in the fortress of his inner being.

The Value of Listening and Communication

Few works reveal the importance of communication and listening better than James Lynch's book, *The Broken Heart.* He shows how lonely, isolated people are far more often the victims of death from all sorts of diseases than those who have human companionship and communication. Human beings literally die when they are cut off from human interaction. And the first step in communication is listening to one another.

Love desires to find out about other human beings. It is interested in the events of the day, the thoughts, desires, fears, even the angers or fantasies of others. If love is genuine, it cares; and caring nearly always involves listening. Louis Evely has stated this well in *That Man Is You:*

> Love must express and communicate itself . . .
>> That's its nature . . .
> When two people begin to love one another,
>> they start telling everything that's happened to
>>> them,
>> every detail of their daily life;
>> they reveal themselves to each other,
>> unbosom themselves and exchange confi-
>>> dences . . .
> God hasn't ceased being Revelation . . .
>> any more than He's ceased being Love.
> He enjoys expressing Himself.
> Since He's Love, He must give Himself,
>> share his secrets . . .
>> communicate with us . . .
>> and reveal himself to anyone who wants to listen.[1]

Without listening there is little communication, and without communication there is little love. Each of us needs desperately to be listened to, to be found by another who can listen to us and love us just as we are.

One of the indications of the small amount of listening there is in our world and even in our Christian society is the high price that psychologists and psychiatrists demand. Bruno Klopfer, the authority on the Rorschach test, once told me that fifty percent of all psychotherapy was only warm, receptive listening. And people are willing to pay from twenty-five to one hundred dollars an hour just to be listened to!

And yet how seldom have we felt truly listened to and with what thirst we long for it! How often have we listened to a friend or a spouse or a parent or a child for an hour without interjecting our own agenda, values and desires? How often have we been able to put aside our own human reactions, our egotism, our wants and wishes and listen to another person for an entire hour?

Klopfer told me a story about the effectiveness of friendly listening. A student of his was taking a course on how to use and interpret the Rorschach inkblot test. As part of his training he was given the assignment of taking an experimental Rorschach on a woman who had been institutionalized in a state hospital in Colorado for five years. She had received both electro-shock and insulin shock therapy. Nothing seemed to help. Her condition had been judged incurable and she was relegated to a custodial ward.

The Rorschach, however, showed some signs of life slumbering within her. Klopfer suggested that the student return to see the woman once a week for a friendly visit and listen to her. The student had had no training in psychotherapy, but he made five visits. On the sixth visit he found that the woman had been judged well enough to be discharged, and she had gone home. Simple listening had been enough to bring about a cure. Such listening certainly need not be limited to those trained in psychotherapy.

There are few things more important for effective human relationships than continued, attentive listening. It is hardly possible to respect others if we have not had the courtesy to listen to them. Listening shows concern for what I am. It is difficult for me to believe that others are interested in me, care for me, love me, unless they have the respect that is shown in listening to me, not only once, but over and over again.

There is a vast difference between letting another person unload and true listening. We can dump our problems at the hairdresser's or at a bar. The only response we get is "poor dear" or "tough luck, buddy." This is not listening. It is a tragic commentary on modern Christianity that such unloading takes place more often at these secular establishments than at church.

So often we assume that we know others quite well. We forget that they change and need to be listened to again and again to find where they are now. Nothing remains totally the same in the world of flux and change, and this is particularly true of human beings. To *keep knowing and loving* others, we need to continue to listen to them. It is strange indeed how often the very people who are closest to us are the very ones to whom we listen the least. This is particularly true within the family.

Real listening is a difficult and demanding discipline. There are few activities harder to keep doing well. We get tired and want someone to take care of us. Late one afternoon a woman came to see me in my office. I asked her how she was, and she answered that she was quite well. I replied that I was happy that she had no serious problems because I was tired after listening to heavy problems all day. The hour continued pleasantly and the woman left. Several years later while visiting her in the hospital I found that she had really come laden with problems that day. Her daughter was pregnant out of wedlock, and she had just come from the doctor's office where she had learned that she had cancer. My concern for myself had kept me from listening when someone needed me. We never know what problems others may carry.

Ten Suggestions on Learning To Listen

If listening is as important as it appears, how can I develop this essential ingredient of love? Learning to listen is a process which takes a long time and can become a way of life. Reflecting back over thirty-five years of trying to listen, I perceive ten different steps for learning to grow in this skill.

1. First of all, I need to learn to cease talking myself. Obviously we cannot listen until we stop talking. And it is hard for most of us human beings to halt our chatter. No member of the body seems to be more difficult to control than the tongue. At times it seems to have a life of its own, a life quite independent of our will and rational control.

Constant chatter is usually a form of shyness. We are too insecure to be silent. A wall of words keeps us insulated from others. If we can talk enough, we can prevent people from getting close to us and avoid real communion with them. Continuous talking achieves the same results as social isolation. It obstructs real contact with other human beings and therefore with life itself.

Continuous talking can also be a supreme form of cowardice and can lead to serious spiritual and psychological difficulties. One of the characters in Charles Williams' novel, *All Hallows Eve,* lost her soul because of her ceaseless, mindless chatter. Her barrage of words kept her bound up in herself and insulated from the saving action of redeeming love.

But what if I am with another person and nothing is said by either of us? I feel so uncomfortable that I fear I may shrivel up and die. However, I have never known any casualties that resulted from being silent with another.

A story is told of a counselor who was visited by a counselee. They greeted each other and then sat down in chairs facing each other. The counselor sat there relaxed, with arms extended and resting on his chair, quietly attentive. Five minutes passed and nothing was said; then twenty passed and still not a word was uttered. Finally the fifty-minute hour was over, and there had been no conversation.

The counselor got up from his chair. The client rose to his feet, strode over to the counselor, extended his hand and said, "You will never know what this hour has meant to me. I did not think anyone could abide my presence for an hour without words."

2. It is one thing to cease talking (necessary as this is as a first step) and quite another matter to learn to listen. Real listening is being silent with another person or group of persons in an active way. It is quietly bearing with others. Some people are silent without being open and active. They are either lost in themselves, dead or asleep. True listeners are those who are quiet and yet sensitive toward others, open, active, receptive and alive, those who do not allow their minds to wander or to daydream. Listening is participating in other lives in a creative and powerful way. It is neither coercive nor overbearing. Listening is one of the best ways to bear the burdens of others.

We need to be silent not only with our lips, but also in our inner being. When we truly listen to others, we are silent inside. We neither agree nor disagree with what is said. We are open and receptive, permitting the others to be what they are, and that freely. Listening gives freedom and does not need to control what is heard, does not need to censor it.

My body language often reveals the quality of my listening. If someone comes to me seeking to be heard, I can easily turn them off and give signs that I do not really want to listen. Eye contact conveys a great number of messages, and dark glasses can be a form of hiding and not wishing to listen. I can sit with my arms folded across my chest. This posture often screams: "Stay away from me!" I can watch the clock or clench my hands. We can give off a thousand cues which tell the other that we are there only because we have to be, and then real listening does not occur.

It is nearly impossible to listen until we have started upon the long road of accepting ourselves. Once we can look at all of us, the good and the evil, once we have been able to put aside our illusions about ourselves, then we can begin to listen because we are not going to be upset or shocked by what we hear. We already know ourselves, and seldom do we find anything more shocking that what we find in the depth of ourselves.

Elizabeth O'Connor puts this well in her book, *Search for Silence.* She tells how often we come to create unreal images of who and what we are. "We come to believe more and more in them. We fashion an unreal self and become enmeshed in the nets of our own labor. It does not take long to begin to think that this self—this idol that we have constructed—is all there is to us. We invent our own legend and come to believe that our salvation lies in perpetuating it. This cuts us off from our real self and gives rise to uneasy, tremulous feelings."[2] Such self-deception also makes it impossible for us to listen to others.

People caught in illusions about themselves cannot even read books with which they disagree. They fight the authors in order to protect their illusion, and so they get little value from what they have read. Listening to others is not so different from listening to books. Many people cannot bear to hear ideas or actions of which they disapprove. They fear that they condone whatever they listen to. And so they dare not listen without reaction, emotional and verbal, without vociferous dissent—as if opinion expressed with emotion offered protection. We need to begin to develop inner security, which comes from loving ourselves, if we are to listen to others. Our very ability to listen is a sign that we are achieving some inner security.

3. Listening involves patience. When we try to force listening, we usually shut it off. Others need to reveal themselves at their own speed in their own way. I listened to one young man at Notre Dame once a week for three school years before he finally trusted me enough to reveal what he considered the deepest stain on his soul.

Listening creates a deeper bond than most of us realize. To break off the listening process can do great damage to others. We assume a certain responsibility for people when we begin to listen to them. There are few things worse than thinking that another truly cares and will listen to us and then finding that he or she could not accept all

74

of us or was no longer interested. Patience and perseverance are elements of loving listening.

Antoine de Saint Exupery illustrates this truth in the opening pages of *The Little Prince:*

"One only understands the things that one tames," said the fox. . . .

"What must I do, to tame you?" asked the little prince.

"You must be very patient," replied the fox. "First you will sit down at a little distance from me—like that—in the grass. I shall look at you out of the corner of my eye, and you will say nothing. Words are the source of misunderstanding. But you will sit a little closer to me, every day. . . . If, for example, you come at four o'clock in the afternoon, then at three o'clock I shall begin to be happy. I shall feel happier and happier as the hour advances. . . ." So the prince tamed the fox. And when the hour of his departure drew near . . . (the fox gave the prince a present of a secret).

"Men have forgotten this truth," said the fox. "But you must never forget it. You become responsible, forever, for what you have tamed. . . ."

One runs the risk of weeping a little if one lets himself be tamed. . . .[3]

And when we are listened to, we are indeed tamed and made members of the human race. Then we know what it means to care and to be cared for.

4. Creative listeners do not always remain silent. Far from it, they respond, reflect, express understanding and empathy. No one has written more profoundly about reflective listening than Carl Rogers in his many excellent books. He shows how important real listening is to all human relationships, to personal growth, to psychotherapy, to education. Reflective listening, to use Rogers' phrase, amplifies and clarifies what the speaker says. It may ask for more details, but always with the intention of finding out

what is within the other person and facilitating what the other wishes to express. Real listening is never artificial or stilted. It is warm, interested, concerned. It seeks to know and to care. It is love in action.

Seldom, however, does a good listener offer quick or easy answers to problems. Jung has remarked that good advice seldom hurts any of us because we so seldom take it seriously. But it can cut off those who are speaking and keep them from getting to their more significant agenda. Listening to another is listening to the other's experience from their point of view.

Real listening requires reflection. We need to process our reactions and words through our thinking and feeling functions. When we speak to another person without thinking about the effect our words may have, we are likely to be thoughtless. One of the meanings of the word thoughtless is inconsiderate. Being inconsiderate seldom conveys love. Thoughtless words can also separate us from the people to whom we wish to listen.

A little pamphlet on listening is used by Reuel Howe at the Institute for Advanced Pastoral Studies. We are reminded in it that for the five hundred most commonly used words in the English language there are over fourteen hundred different meanings. This means an average of nearly three different meanings for each word. No wonder we often need clarification if we are going to understand others and truly listen. In the same pamphlet are reprinted some specific listening techniques from a paper by R. K. Burns of the Industrial Relations Center of the University of Chicago,[4] and they are so helpful that I pass them on to the reader.

One of the poorest and least effective modes of communication is the lecture where there is no time left for questions. It is futile and nearly immoral to lecture to people. Unless there are questions, we never know when we have been understood. Early in my teaching at Notre Dame I was impressed with this truth. I went to Notre Dame realizing that most of the students would have been trained in Thomistic theology, and I geared my presentations to this understanding. A Dutch priest was in the class,

TYPES	PURPOSE	EXAMPLES
1. Clarifying	1. To get at additional facts 2. To help him explore all sides of a problem.	1. "Can you clarify this?" 2. "Do you mean this?" 3. "Is this the problem as you see it now?"
2. Restatement	1. To check our meaning and interpretation with his. 2. To show you are listening and that you understand what he is saying. 3. To encourage him to analyze other aspects of matter being considered and to discuss it with you.	1. "As I understand it then your plan is . . . " 2. "This is what you have decided to do and the reasons are . . . "
3. Neutral	1. To convey that you are interested and listening. 2. To encourage the person to continue talking.	1. "I see." 2. "Uh-huh." 3. "That's very interesting." 4. "I understand."
4. Reflective	1. To show that you understand how he feels about what he is saying. 2. To help person to evaluate and temper his own feelings as expressed by someone else.	1. "You feel that . . . " 2. "It was a shocking thing as you saw it." 3. "You felt that you didn't get a fair shake."
5. Summarizing	1. To bring all the discussion into focus in terms of a summary. 2. To serve as a springboard for further discussion on a new aspect of problem.	1. "These are the key ideas you have expressed." 2. "If I understand how you feel about the situation . . . "

and did not seem to understand anything that I was saying. Finally I realized that he had been raised in a totally different theological framework and so almost nothing I said made any sense. Once I realized this, I could express what I wanted to say within his existential framework. Through this experience I realized clearly that a form of feedback is essential for communications; and receiving feedback is, of course, a form of listening.

5. Listening is an art for which some people have a gift. It is also a skill which can be learned, and it is a discipline which needs to be taught and practiced. How can I acquire this skill and discipline in order to enhance the gifts I may have?

We have schools in which we teach the use of language, the understanding of numbers and mathematics, classes for learning music and even classes for playing bridge. And yet we have but few schools or classes in listening. We assume that we can all listen. Unfortunately what we assume to be true is usually false. Except for a few people who are gifted in listening as Mozart was in music, most of us need to learn to listen.

The most effective classes in listening that I have encountered took place as part of the education program of St. Luke's Parish, where I was rector for twenty years. Dr. Ollie Backus, who inaugurated the program, said quite bluntly that it was hypocrisy to speak of Christian love where there were no classes in listening; and so she instituted these classes which have continued in the parish to this day. No one was permitted to teach in the carefully designed educational program who had not taken part in these listening classes.

The classes consisted of eight students and an instructor. Carl Rogers' book *On Becoming a Person* was used as a text. However, the main assignment was not just reading the text, but a practice session. The eight students were divided into four pairs. Each pair spent an hour in which they listened to each other before a tape recorder. First of all, one person would talk for fifteen to twenty minutes about some significant issue in his or her life and the other person listened. Then the roles were reversed and the former listener held forth on something important in his or her life. After this session they listened to the tapes and discussed them. They would share where they felt listened to and where they did not feel listened to. Thus each of them knew when they were listening and when they had cut the other person off and were not listening. *The only way to tell whether or not we are listening is to find out if the other person* feels *listened to.* Listening, like love, is transitive. It does not take place unless the other experiences it also.

The tapes were then brought to the class session and played there, and the instructor and the class members would make suggestions on how both of them could be better listeners. Many of those who took these classes reported that they found them one of the most helpful learning experiences of their lives.

There are many places where one can find a listening class and receive training in listening. Even people who think that they are good listeners often find that they can learn a great deal in such a situation. I wonder if it is possible truly to profess Christianity and the practice of love if we have not tried in some way to sharpen our skills in listening. I wonder if a Christian parish church is offering genuine Christian education if it does not provide training in listening skills and offer listening classes for children and adults.

Reflective listening can be misused and become a parody of genuine listening. Like any other communication skill, when this practice is used as a bloodless technique it becomes ridiculous. The story is told of a distressed person who came to a counselor for help. He sat down in a chair and said: "I feel very depressed." The therapist replied, "You do feel very depressed, don't you?" Then the client went on: "I feel so depressed that I feel like jumping out of that window." This statement was reflected back by these words: "You feel so terribly miserable that you think it would be an easy way out to jump out of the window." At that point the depressed person got up and went to the window and jumped out. The counselor went to the window and after his client hit the sidewalk said, "Plop!" Some attempts at totally objective listening are as sick as this story!

6. Listening often involves sharing ourselves. Some schools of thought in counseling suggest that the counselors should share nothing of themselves. They are to be strictly impersonal. My experience is quite different. I have found that when I am most truly me, I listen the most effectively and convey genuine caring. Often people who come for counseling are quite frightened (indeed most of us are, at some level in our being). We wonder if anyone can or will ever understand us. Since we have not been listened to, we often think that we alone are mixed up, confused and peculiar.

My woundedness at this point is frequently my greatest asset. I often say to the person, "Don't be afraid. I am not looking down my long and bony nose at a case. I, too, have suffered and have my neuroses. Welcome into the club, the fellowship of *morbus sacer,* holy woundedness." How often I have seen this approach put others at ease. Then I can ask people what is on their minds and hearts, and the floodgates often open. Of course this sharing of myself is to be used only to put the other at ease. If I find that I am using it to unburden myself, then I need to find a professional listener to care for *my* need. We must be very careful not to share more than the other person can bear or cares to hear. The troubled person coming to be listened to should not become my therapist.

No one has written more sensitively on the use of woundedness in the loving process than Henri Nouwen in his book, *The Wounded Healer.* He points out that "making one's own wounds a source of healing, therefore, does not call for a sharing of superficial personal pains but for a constant willingness to see one's own pain and suffering as rising from the depth of the human condition which all men share. . . . A shared pain is no longer paralyzing but mobilizing, when understood as a way of liberation. When we become aware that we do not have to escape our pains, but that we can mobilize them into a common search for life,

80

those very pains are transformed from expressions of despair into signs of hope. . . . "⁵

Nouwen illustrates this truth in his chapter "Ministry by a Lonely Minister" by citing an old legend from the Talmud:

> Rabbi Yoshua ben Levi came upon Elijah the prophet while he was standing at the entrance of a fellow rabbi's cave. He asked Elijah, "When will the Messiah come?"
> Elijah replied,
> "Go and ask him yourself."
> "Where is he?"
> "Sitting at the gates of the city."
> "How shall I know him?"
> "He is sitting among the poor covered with wounds. The others unbind all their wounds at the same time and then bind them up again. But he unbinds one at a time and binds it up again, saying to himself, "Perhaps I shall be needed: if so I must always be ready so as not to delay for a moment."⁶

7. Only rarely are we allowed into the deeper levels of the human soul until we have listened to the more superficial levels of other people. We may need to listen first of all to someone's petty concerns and interests and desires and hopes. We may listen to descriptions of events which have been meaningful and tragic to that person. We may listen to complaints about aches and pains, what one wag has described as "the organ recital."

As we bear with other human beings with their pettiness and littleness, then we often hear a tentative statement of something more. We pick up a thread of something within others that they may not even know is there. We discover that we are being led slowly and gently into the deeper and more vulnerable levels of the soul. The novel experience of truly being listened to has fostered hope. The person feels that perhaps there is another who cares after all, a person who will try to understand. Certainly there is little reason for us to believe this possibility until someone tries to listen to us. Listening to me may even open me to myself. Often when I have been well listened to, I realize things about myself I did not know before.

If we pass these first tentative tests of our acceptance and listen, then sometimes a dam breaks and the whole human being pours fourth—the entire person with guilts and faults and sins, with feelings of despair, inadequacy, loneliness, self-hatred, self-judgment and inner pain.

It is difficult for most of us to bear this flood. We all have these dark areas in our own souls, and these begin to throb in sympathy. To listen to the agony of others often stirs up our own. Jung listened to so much darkness that he found it necessary to go away one month in four in order to discharge the poison he had picked up in listening.

Yet if we do not listen to this dark side of others, we seldom see these people in depth. They remain for us like a child's painting, with no shadow or perspective. One friend who had revealed his worst to me (and it was pretty bad) decided that henceforth he should carry his burdens himself. When we met again under these conditions we did not meet at all. Later he realized what had happened, and he wrote saying that now he truly understood that we only know one another when we share our darkness as well as our joy and well-being.

8. And then often we experience a still deeper level of sharing. Students at Notre Dame would often come in to see me bringing a book to discuss. Soon I discovered that the book was only a ruse. They wanted to talk about themselves to someone who would listen. We went through superficial concerns, then discussed the problems with parents (for all of us have authority problems hidden deep within us) and the problems with sex (I have never known a person who had no sexual confusions), and finally we came to the deepest and most secret level of all. Often they revealed this level only at graduation time, as they were about to leave. They would come like Nicodemus at night and tell me of their religious experiences and their desire to be priests and give their total lives to Christ. *People seldom reveal this level of themselves to us unless they know*

that we see the soul as holy and that we are open to all of them. Raymond Moody reports that people with near-death experiences will only relate their stories to those who are open to this possibility. Andrew Greeley notes in his research that many people have deep mystical experiences, but will not reveal them lest they be mocked. A flippant attitude often screens out this level of self-disclosure.

When we listen on this level, we often hear strange echoes, see unearthly lights and catch strains of the mysterious music of the soul. Beyond the darkness of the soul lies a beauty we never dreamed existed in this mortal world. Then it is easy and natural for us to love the other person. In this deepest level of the human psyche we discover the spirit of the living Christ, the Holy Spirit, the shekina or glorious blaze of the Father. As we pass with courage through the demonic darkness, then suddenly the veil lifts and we find that within another human being we have communion with God in Triune mystery.

It makes no difference how depraved or how simple the others are; there in the central fortress of the soul is a secret oratory in which the Divine Lover dwells. This is why we are all so incalculably valuable and why we may never use others as means, but only as ends. There is something divine in every human being. When we are listening with total openness, we can come to communion with that reality.

Listening on this level, we come to love those who have revealed themselves to us, for we experience them as God-bearers. We often are awestruck by the mystery of the human soul which carries such a spirit within it. Indeed, I doubt if any of us are ever ushered into the deepest recesses of another soul unless our lives and actions express some of this awe. Something instinctive in us keeps this level closed except for those who have developed this kind of reverence, those who can listen in holy awe. Obviously when we feel this way about others we do not repeat what they have told us to anyone. What we have heard becomes our holy secret. Of course, we seldom hear much from others unless they know that we can and will keep their confidence.

Listening on this level is a kind of prayer. When we listen in this way we penetrate through the human part of our being with its darkness and come to hear the Spirit of God which dwells in each of us. Real listening can be a religious experience. Sometimes when I have listened deeply to another, I have the same sense of awe as when I am alone in the church at night and the votive lights flicker against the arched windows. I have entered into a holy place and have communed with the heart of Being itself.

What we experience of the Divine through other human beings confirms the knowledge of God which we have had directly in our own souls. Seldom do we develop the capacity for listening to the still small voice of God until we have first learned to open ourselves to other human beings. Rudolf Steiner put it well: "Only to those, who by selfless listening train themselves to be really receptive within, in stillness, unmoved by personal opinion or feeling, only to such can the higher beings speak. . . . As long as one hurls any personal opinion or feeling against the speaker to whom one must listen, the beings of the spiritual world remain silent."[7]

9. There are a few simple rules which often help us to listen to one another. Few people can talk about their deepest feelings unless there is privacy and time. Listening requires a private and quiet place.

Sometimes I talk with friends who are trained in counseling. We listen to each other. But this requires that I have my uninterrupted time to share myself, and then when I am finished I offer the same kind of listening time to the other person. Unless we come to some such arrangement, we both leave frustrated, often feeling used rather than understood.

Time for listening should be limited to an hour except in the most unusual circumstances. What needs to be said can be said in an hour, and often the psyche waits until the last moment to reveal itself. I have found at conferences where my time is limited that I can often hear as much in thirty minutes as in the ordinary fifty-minute hour.

10. Whenever I argue or interrupt another person I usually find that a sensitive spot in my own being has been

struck. These attitudes usually put a stop to fruitful communication. Almost never will I pass judgment on the other person, nor will I give advice unless I am asked. When I do judge, it is only to show the dangers into which certain actions can lead the other person. I do not judge the person. When I give unsolicited advice it is because I see pitfalls the other has not seen, pitfalls which might destroy that person. In listening I try not to be overinvolved or to react emotionally in response (positively or negatively) to the feelings of others. When I jump to conclusions I usually jump to the wrong ones. Listening usually means holding my own conclusions in abeyance until others come to their conclusions. My task in listening is the same as in loving— to enable others to grow, to take responsibility for their own lives, to form their own value system, and to come to their own full potential by their own choice.

To Whom?

And to whom should we listen? The answer is very simple. We need to listen to everyone whom we would care for or love. And whom should we love? At this point we will want to establish some priorities. To whom do we owe the greatest responsibility? Establishment of priorities is something that we seldom do without reflection and some kind of journal keeping.

Our listening enables us to love, and our love gives us the opportunity to enable others to come to their potential. To whom do we owe the most? To husband or wife? To our children? To our neighbors? Friends? Employers? Employees? To the clerk in the variety store, the boy who delivers the newspaper, the acquaintance? To the person whom we pass in the street or the child sobbing in a subway, the stranger? To the one who has hurt us or whom we have hurt, the enemy?

If I had one thing to do over in my life with regard to my loving and my listening, I would have clarified my priorities and placed my wife and my children at the top of the list. God has given me these special people as primary objects for care and love. As a married priest, there has been real tension between my responsibility to my family on the one hand and to parishioners and those who have knocked on my door in the middle of the night on the other hand. How can I give love with a clear conscience to those outside the family circle until I have given it within that circle? One advantage of celibate religious life is that it relieves this tension. However, if the celibate does not give love within the rectory or religious community, then the love given to others can also be tinged with the same hypocrisy.

6

Loving the Family
and Those Who Love Us

The evidence is in and it is overwhelming. The most potent factor in the development of children is the quality of the family life in which they are raised. It is quite obvious and understandable that the attitudes and values of children spring from their family life. Love breeds love, violence stimulates violence, indifference fosters indifference and apathy. It is also understandable that mental stability and health are the product of a loving environment just as mental illness is often the tragic result of a lack of love during the first years of life. Even physical stature and bodily stamina are influenced by the kind of family life we have had and the amount of love we have received. Babies who are not fondled in nurseries, even the most bacterially sterile, may wither and die with a strange disease known as *mirasmus*. James Lynch summarizes all this data in his telling and important book, *The Broken Heart*.

Psychotherapy is professional friendship. Its main task is to provide an environment in which those who did not receive genuine concern and care as they were growing up may receive it at a later date. Real friendship and genuine community provide a healing and sustaining environment, fostering the life and growth of us human beings.

For nearly forty years I have been listening to people in trouble as pastor, teacher and counselor. For the last twenty years I have been a professional marriage, family and child counselor as well as a priest. In the parish I served in southern California we developed a psychological clinic because we found that so many people were hurt and warped and wanted to straighten out their lives. I have listened to thousands of people, and one fact emerges. Few people live satisfactory lives, have satisfactory homes and marriages or make satisfying relationships with others. Listening to marriage disputes is often like listening to the sandbox squabblings of three-year-olds. The statistics on marriage failure are staggering. In Los Angeles County there are many weeks in which there are more divorces than marriages. Were it not for remarriage and those coming from outside, few people would still be married there. In California one marriage out of every two breaks up in divorce. The national average is one divorce in every three or four marriages.

Husbands are often against wives and wives against husbands. Parents find children incorrigible and children reject and cut off relations with parents. This is the state of affairs among us in the Western world. *And the worst part of the tragedy for Christians is that these statistics are nearly as true among them as among non-Christians. What is the trouble?*

Jesus and Intimacy

If there was one point at which Jesus may have underestimated human frailty, it may have been in his failure to see the difficulties his followers might have in their intimate relationships. Jesus simply assumed that we would love our families, our children, our wives, husbands, brothers and sisters, parents and grandparents, our friends and intimates—even as the good heathen do. He was quite clear in what is reported in the Sermon on the Mount: "If you love only those who love you, what reward can you expect? Surely the tax-gatherers do as much as that. And if you greet only your brothers, what is there extraordinary about that? Even the heathen do as much" (Matthew 5:46–47).

It never seemed to occur to Jesus that he would have to tell us to love those who love us. And yet, looking at the Christian family life today, we often do not even see Christians working at this primary level of love. How has it come about that modern-day Christians are often not as advanced in loving those closest to them as the heathen and tax-collectors, the harlots and sinners of Christ's time? How has it come about that often we are no better than the heathen in our family life?

In order to answer this difficult question, we shall first of all look at Jesus' attitude toward intimate relationships and toward women, children and family life. We shall then offer some practical and specific suggestions on *how* we can love our families. After dealing briefly with the problem of dealing with our hostilities in close relationships, we shall conclude with observations about loving the aging and with a personal account of my learning to love one member of my family.

The ancient heathen were taught to love their friends and families with a burning love and to hate their enemies with a determined hatred. They worked at both endeavors. Heathen friends were forever and could be counted on until hell froze over. After Christianity became the accepted religion of the Western world, our Christian forebears were taught that they should not hate. This was difficult for the best of Christians in the golden age of Christianity, but then came the barbarian invasions and the mass baptisms which produced skin-deep Christians. Many of these people who tried not to hate simply repressed their hatred and no longer looked at it. The hatred dropped down into the depth of them, was forgotten and ignored in the unconscious. Then like yeast it fermented and worked autonomously. And when it exploded, as it nearly always did at one time or another, it often came out upon those who were the nearest, upon those closest to them, upon their loved ones. Sometimes these inner hates came out against the Jews or infidels. The same kinds of reaction have continued from that day to this. Except in time of war our families and loved ones often receive the treatment which was once reserved only for one's enemies.

Jesus and Equality of Male and Female

The followers of Jesus of Nazareth have also been saddled with two other unique ideas—the idea of the equality and equal value of women, and the idea of the value of children just as children. For this reason Christian marriage and family life requires a mutuality and respect which are difficult for even the most mature and conscious human beings. Family life based on genuine mutuality differs basically from family life in which one member or another is the titular or actual head of the house. The latter arrangement short-circuits mutual concern for one another and avoids the stress of mutual relationship.

The ancient world of which Jesus was a part believed that men were the heads of each household. Women existed to bear children and to minister to the needs of men. Women were not believed to be men's equals physically, mentally, morally or religiously. Since they were considered inferior to men, it followed that men felt that they should rule the family with complete authority.

Children were often not worth much in this patriarchal family structure unless, of course, they were male. And even male children might be sold into slavery if economic conditions were bad. On the whole children were considered valuable only as they grew up; they were treated as merely potential human beings.

Jesus did not agree with this view of family life and relationships. It did not accord with what he knew about human beings and about God himself. No one has had more to do with the breakdown of this purely masculine attitude toward the family than Jesus of Nazareth. Just as his teaching about the basic moral equality of human beings and their equal worth before God finally bore fruition in the abandonment of slavery, so too his teaching about the family would ultimately end masculine domination of family

90

life. It took eighteen hundred years before his ideas about slavery took root, and his ideas about women and children have still not taken root among many Christians.[1]

The importance that Jesus attributed to children was simply not shared by the world in which Jesus lived. One towering greatness of Jesus may be seen in his divergence from popular opinion, divergence which later generations have come to see as based on psychological, moral and religious truth. When some mothers wanted Jesus to bless their little children, the disciples' irritation expressed the current attitude: a person engaged in religiously significant tasks should not be pestered with such petty annoyances as children (Mark 10:13ff).

Jesus' reaction in this story is instructive. He was angry—and he let his indignation show. "Let the children come to me," he said. "Do not try to stop them; for the kingdom of God belongs to such as these. I tell you, whoever does not accept the kingdom of God like a child will never enter it." And then Jesus put his arms around them, laid his hands upon them and blessed them.

These words reflect his strong reaction. They convey the same feeling found in the account of the disciples' argument over which of them was the greatest. Jesus settled this dispute by bringing a child over in front of them and, with his arms around the youngster, saying, "Whoever receives this child in my name receives me; and whoever receives me, receives him who sent me." Then Jesus went on to speak his conviction that to corrupt children is the worst kind of evil. Using, perhaps, the strongest language ever recorded of him, he told those around him: "As for the man who leads astray one of these little ones who have faith, it would be better for him to be thrown into the sea with a millstone around his neck." It took a long time before these words were heeded in matters of education and restriction of child labor, even in Christian countries.

It was not only in China and India that unwanted babies were put outside to die of exposure. (And not even Buddha, Confucius or Lao-Tse thought enough about it to teach anything different.) The Hellenistic world in which Jesus lived routinely did away with children who were weak, unfit or unwanted. It was commonplace to abandon babies, particularly girls, in the wilds until they died from cold and hunger.

In singular fashion the teachings of Jesus make it clear that children have value in themselves. Indeed, they may well be closer to God than adults. Anything, therefore, which hinders, wounds or corrupts a child is evil and deserving of the firmest rebuke. This applies to parents as well as pimps and pirates. The primary value of the family is to nurture and protect children; and because of this, it possesses incalculable value. Anything, therefore, which strikes at the solidarity of the family is dangerous and evil.

The divorced woman is certainly no longer equipped to care for her children in the same way that a married woman is. Jesus' radical statements about divorce probably spring in part from his high valuation of children, women and family life. Even among Jews in the time of Christ a man could divorce his wife for truly trivial reasons by handing her a bill of divorcement. In many cases this action condemned her to a life of prostitution—one of the few professions open to women in the ancient world. Women had few rights and values of their own. They were dependent on men for their worth.

Jesus alone among the great religious leaders of the world saw women as equal in value to men. Even the Jewish rabbis, who did esteem children (far more than most other religious mentors), set women on a definitely inferior level. Confucius advised the religious man to shun women or to keep them in their place. Buddha spoke of women as one of the snares which the man bent on religious enlightenment must avoid. He himself left his wife and family when the pull of the religious way became strong. In the Hindu classic, the *Ramayana*, the hero finally leaves his beloved wife so that he can tend to his soul.

Jesus, however, counted women among his constant companions. Contrary to the custom of his day and the ways of other religious leaders, he spoke specifically to women on many occasions and treated them with the same respect that he gave to men. Evidently women did not threaten him, for he dealt with them just as he dealt with men. This was a radical attitude for a rabbi in the first century. It was to take many, many years before this attitude became current among Christian religious leaders. It is no wonder that the women's liberation movement often takes such a dim view of Christianity. The writings of influential spiritual authors such as St. Ignatius of Loyola or Adolphe Tanquerey reveal little of Jesus' attitude on this matter.

Furthermore, the values which are often associated with women and may even be instinctive with them had been largely overlooked in patriarchal society. In this area also, Jesus' attitude was a radical turnabout. He saw the kindness, mercy, self-giving and love which so often characterize motherhood and womanhood as essential to life as it ought to be lived.

Family life as a cooperative venture between equals is only possible where women and children are esteemed as highly as men. Often their values and functions differ from those of men, but they are just as important. Polygamy is unthinkable as a general Christian practice. Few women really want to share a man, yet polygamy has been common in China and India and in all the lands of Islam. Mohammed expressly set down the conditions for having up to four wives. In cultures where women and children do not have individual, separate value, family life as we know it is literally impossible. According to Jesus, women and children are to be equal partners, cooperating freely and not being forced into servitude by the power of men. They have the same right to joy and satisfaction as men. They are no longer just housekeepers (whether in a work house or a house of pleasure). They are no longer servants.

Although most of what Jesus said about women, children and family life is held in principle by most Western culture, the actual practice is far different. Marilyn French's important, angry and shocking book, *The Women's Room*, shows how inferior the position of women is in much of modern American society. My experience as a marriage counselor bears out her thesis. Men who think that women have an equal share of our society should read this book. Most women don't need to read it.

Jesus, however, never intended to turn the world or

93

the family over to the feminine by itself. He also stressed the traditional masculine values and he *lived them out*. It is strange how often we miss the masculine side of Jesus of Nazareth and do not listen to what he said. He spoke of God as Father—and sometimes a demanding and strict one. Jesus himself was a man who could endure forty days and nights of fasting in the wilderness, who could put up with rejection and contempt, who could live with no place to lay his head. He stood without wincing before the Sanhedrin and the Roman governor. He took their buffeting and flogging without a word. He withstood the torture of crucifixion with incredible silence. He was a strong man and he could argue with astounding clarity. He was afraid of no one. Often he spoke with disarming frankness about the tragedy which violence breeds now and hereafter, about the separation of the sheep from the goats. He spoke openly about the vices of the scribes and the Pharisees which were minor compared to those of the pagans.

Jesus had unsettling words to say about the family: "Who is my mother? Who are my brothers?" Then he looked around him at those who were gathered there and added, "Here are my mother and my brothers. Whoever does the will of God is my brother, my sister, my mother" (Mark 3:33). Jesus knew that there could be no real family relationships unless people became conscious enough to choose for themselves. They have to be able to break with the past if they are to follow God and God's way for the family.

On another occasion Jesus was even more blunt. "I have come to bring division. For from now on, five members of a family will be divided, three against two and two against three; father against son and son against father, mother against daughter and daughter against mother, mother against son's wife and son's wife against her mother-in-law" (Matthew 10:34–35). These were harsh words for the Jewish people who expected obedience in these relationships and who learned that they must give love and honor to parents because their ancestors had loved and honored in this way. Now Jesus told them it was more im-

94

portant to become father or mother in a *real*, balanced relationship than just to follow a traditional role.

Jesus knew that women cannot be real women where men are not real men. Nothing destroys womanhood more completely than having no genuine men to take up their side of *equal* partnership. Women need men as much as men need women, and they want them. The most persistent and irrefutable complaint I hear from women in counseling sessions is that men are not strong or willing enough to relate to them or to take their stand in life.

So often we human beings spend our time looking for the person whom it is easy to love, the cheerful, pleasant, attractive person. Is not our task more to be loving so that people around us can become pleasant and creative and fulfilled? Love can usually create love in those in close relationships unless there are deep wounds and hurts which keep a person shielded from love. One of the most important purposes of psychotherapy is to help people through these roadblocks to love so that they can come alive in their intimate relationships. Love usually engenders itself in those around us. Its influence, however, is often slow; and it takes weeks and years for its mysterious power to come to fruition.

How Do We Love Those Who Love Us?

Love which is merely general and universal is not love at all. Loving everyone is a great ideal, but a hollow one. A seminary student came to me several years ago wondering how he could love everyone as one of his professors had suggested. It took several years before he realized that he could not love humankind in general until he learned to love individuals, and one individual in particular. After years of effort he allowed himself to love one person, and life opened up to him and his neurosis healed. In many religious orders there used to be a rule against particular friendships. There were reasons for this rule, but often it resulted in a community in which there was little love. Our task, as we have stated earlier, is to give specific, concrete expression to universal love. There is no better place to begin than with those who are close to us—family members (spouse, children and parents), friends, community members, roommates. How do I love those around me? One would hardly think that we need to answer the question, but looking at the record of marriage failure in our Western culture, the answer to this question is not as obvious as we might assume.

My first suggestion is very simple. We need to set a priority on loving those around us. Jung once met a very holy man. He was impressed and thought that he might have to change his life—that is, until he met the man's wife. Then he saw that the man had projected all of his darkness on his wife. She was a tissue of neurosis and suffering, and Jung decided that he need not mend his own ways. This man was not clear on his priorities of loving. His inner "holiness" was more important to him than loving his wife. Seldom do I clarify my priorities until I stop, take time and write what my present priorities are and what I think they should be. I have discussed this practice in my book on journal keeping, *Adventure Inward*.

All human societies provide social support and protection for families and intimate social groups. Within these situations people can be free to love and be loved. In circumstances where we might expect to find love and yet receive none, we are not just let down into a neutral limbo; we are often poisoned and may actually be destroyed. There is no finer discussion of the power of love than Van der Post's novel, *The Face Beside the Fire*. He tells the story of a woman and the husband she had ceased to love: "Slowly she is poisoning Albert. . . . The poison . . . is found in no chemist's book. . . . It is a poison brewed from all the words, the delicate, tender, burning trivialities and petty endearments she's never used—but would have spoken if she'd truly loved him."[2] Even when we don't feel loving we can act in a loving way, and that *is* love. Until we begin to see that our loving is a transforming power, we seldom put proper value upon it. What I truly believe about love is better shown by how I act toward those around me than in what I may write in a theological essay on love.

My second suggestion is simply to express our natural ordinary feelings of affection and warmth when we do feel them. We need not be afraid of expressing concern and caring. Many people I know are quite able to share their negative and hostile feelings, but feel it is somehow immoral to show loving and positive movements of the heart. One of the reasons that anger and criticism are so hard for us to take from loved ones is that often these are the only expressions we hear from them.

There is a lovely story about an Iowa farmer who had been married for twenty years. He chafed under his wife's constant complaint that he did not tell her that he loved her. One Sunday after church at dinner his wife again complained. He rose from the table, stood erect and said: "My dear, when I married you twenty years ago I told you that I loved you; if it changes, I will let you know." When I tell this story at conferences there is nearly always a burst of laughter. The laughter betrays the fact that this kind of atmosphere is found in many, many marriages.

Back in the fourth century St. Ambrose wrote a book on the duty of clergy and how they might grow in Christian love. His advice is as practical today as then for all of us:

> It gives a very great impetus to mutual love if one shows love in return to those who love us and proves that one does not love them less than oneself is loved, especially if one shows it by the proof that a faithful friendship gives. What is so likely to win favour as gratitude? What more natural than to love one who loves us? What so implanted and so impressed on men's feelings as the wish to let another, by whom we want to be loved, know that we love him? Well does the wise man say: "Loose thy money for thy brother and thy friend," and again, "I will not be ashamed to defend a friend, neither will I hide myself from him."[3]

And in discussing the popularity of King David, Ambrose remarked: "Who would not have loved him, when they saw how dear he was to his friends? For as he truly loved his friends, so he thought that he was loved as much in return by his own friends. Because of his love to his friends, people put David above their own families and children."

There is no more important rule in creating growth in love than to be aware of and to express the warmth, caring, and closeness that we feel. There is a story about the childhood of Origen, one of the great theologians of the early Christian church, which tells of his father's *expressed* love, a love that may well explain something of Origen's later greatness. Each night as his father came home, he would enter the room where the child lay sleeping and there he would kiss the child's naked breast, saying that this "was the temple of the Holy Spirit and he was never nearer that Spirit than when he imprinted those kisses there." You may think that this is a little overdone, but this father was not just a sentimental peasant; he was a courageous Christian martyr. He knew and expressed the truth that children who have not known this kind of tenderness and affection seldom grow up into persons capable of independence and love.

Another way of showing love is by simple acts of kindness and thoughtfulness, acts which are sacramental of our love. There is no child who does not appreciate a little gift from the father or mother returning home from a trip, *the gifts as well as the hugs.* There is no woman who does not appreciate a bouquet of flowers and no man who does not appreciate his slippers laid out for him after a hard day. There is no woman who does not appreciate help with dishes at night, and no man who does not appreciate sharing his concerns and interests with a listening spouse. But how seldom we perform these sacramental acts. Why? Because we have so seldom been treated this way ourselves.

In marriage counseling I hear many people complain that they are simply taken for granted. The husbands seldom remember anniversaries or birthdays; they seldom take wives out to dinner or express their love in concrete ways. Then I hear the husbands complain that they are treated as though they were nothing but a bank account.

One problem is that we do not stop and think about the other. I would again call attention to the journal as a means to help us pause and reflect, really think about the other spouse or the children, one by one. What would make them happy? What action of ours would express our love? How seldom do we ever stop to think of these things?

All of us human beings are insecure. At times all of us feel that we are unlovable. Nearly all of us need some little display of affection and interest in us to give us value and worth. And then we get so caught up in our own worthlessness that we don't minister to anyone else. As we try to love ourselves, we are freed to begin to be able to look at the needs of others and reach out to them. And then as we give love, we are more likely to receive it. Usually in the matter of love we receive in somewhat the same measure as we give.

Two negative practices which can destroy years of working at love and caring are sarcasm and ridicule. They cut off the stem which connects us to our worth. Humor is seldom funny at another's expense. How easy to strike out at a husband or wife or child or parent when we are in a corner or feel belittled. *Sarcasm and ridicule are never instruments of love.* This is as true of teachers, employers or co-workers in an office as it is of parents. Again we usually treat our children as we have been treated, and treat our partners in marriage as we saw our parents treat each other. I have talked with thousands of people. Only a few, no more than ten percent, felt that their childhood homes were places where the springs of love flowed freely. If love is to begin to flow in our society, we need to break out of past patterns and begin to express our caring.

The Power of Touch

One touch may convey more than a thousand words. Can you imagine two people living together in the same house for many years and supposedly loving one another and never touching each other? It is unthinkable. Touch expresses a deeper level of feeling and sharing than words or

99

sacramental actions. It is the giving of ourselves to each other. How important this human contact is in conveying the feeling of caring and love!

James Lynch tells of his experiments with patients in the intensive care units in a hospital. In *The Broken Heart* he describes how he noticed that monitoring devices showed an improvement in patients with heart ailments each time the nurse came in to take their pulse. This simple touch seemed to bring a calmer rhythm to badly damaged hearts. He tells of similar experiments with dogs. It has been shown that monkeys brought up with surrogate terry cloth mothers are sickly and are unable to have normal sexual relationships as they grow up. Human babies sometimes die when they are not cuddled.

At the University of Notre Dame many students complained about the lack of touch they experience at home. Brilliant, capable young men in their early twenties would ask: "Why didn't my father ever touch me?" In the next chapter we shall look at some of the reasons why so many of us are afraid of touch. One very brilliant and healthy young man told me that the only time he can remember being touched by his father was when he was spanked. This is the prostitution of touch.

Again we are likely to perpetuate the patterns of family life with which we were raised. When I was a child I was very clumsy and often spilled things at the table. My father would go into a rage. I swore that I would never treat anyone like that, and yet when I had my own child I treated her in the same way until I realized what I was doing. We seldom move out of old patterns until we see that they are wrong, break them, and put other actions in their place.

There is a current fad among some conservative Christians to expound on the value of the switch and physical punishment. Dr. James Dobson speaks of the value of spanking in his recent book *The Strong-Willed Child*. It does not seem to occur to him that there are other ways than physical punishment to convey discipline. He is also naive about the maturity of adults who administer such punishment. Few of us are mature enough to administer punishment to any other person with objectivity. The law takes a dim view of our administering physical punishment in nearly every circumstance. Such practices certainly should not be encouraged.

The Old Testament is no more the final word on child raising than it is on astronomy. I want to make myself very, very clear. I am not saying that children do not need guidance, correction and limits. What I am saying is that most adults give "correction" to children when they are angry, and when this is coupled with physical punishment it is almost unbelievably destructive. What it teaches is that violence is good and might makes right. These are hardly Christian values. Can we even imagine Jesus of Nazareth blowing up and beating a child? Physical punishment of a child by an adult is usually a sign of the adult's feeling of impotence or not thinking that there is any other way to accomplish correction. There are other ways, but they take time and patience.

Several years ago I saw a Russian movie told from a child's point of view and filmed from the eye level of a five-year-old. How different the world looks from this perspective! How big adults look! No wonder we have stories about giants. Little children live in a world of giants, giants who hold everything in their hands. When these giants get angry and strike out, the world of children becomes primordial chaos.

Some educators from a diocesan school system were taking graduate courses at Notre Dame in the program where I taught. A survey revealed that their schools seemed to be effective in teaching nearly everything but religion. Thus they came to study the teaching of religion. We discovered that corporal punishment was still used in their schools. Indeed the diocesan office prescribed the length and thickness and width of the leather strap used in such punishment. We realized that there was nothing in the teaching of Jesus to justify this way of conveying love. Love taught by harshness engenders harshness, not love. I have heard no more than one in a hundred counselees extolling the benefits of physical punishment which they received. Usually I find that it only produces alienation, bitterness, resentment and a sense of valuelessness. And

101

please remember that I am not saying children do not need any limits or correction, for the most unloved child and the most insecure child is the one who is given no direction at all.

When Jesus healed the sick, he usually touched them, laid hands upon them. There is something healing in the touch, something sacramental in the giving of ourselves and more than ourselves. The healing sacrament of anointing or laying-on-of-hands is touch raised to the sacramental level, as the Eucharist is the sacramental use of eating and drinking. Touch can heal, sustain or destroy. It is a powerful instrument and one which needs to be wisely used.

An experience told me by a psychiatrist friend expresses the importance of touch beyond question. He had been working for a long time with a woman whose condition did not seem to improve. And then suddenly she recovered and did not need to come any longer. Sometime later they met at a social gathering. My friend studied her face quietly for a moment, and then asked, "Would you tell me what it was that made you well? Was it anything that I did?" And with a quick smile, she told him, "Oh, I thought you knew. Remember when my son was in the contagious diseases ward in the hospital? I was standing waiting in the corridor and you stopped to ask me how he was doing. You put your hand on my shoulder, and I knew that you really cared. It was then that I started to get better."

Time, Listening and Love

As we have already shown, we cannot love those we do not listen to. This is particularly true in family life and among those who are close to us. And this requires spending time with those whom we would love and setting up conditions where communication can flow freely and naturally. Communication is the goal of listening, and communication is necessary for human life, growth and happiness.

Those times that the family spends together, in outings, holidays and sports, are of great value. However, if we truly care about others or want to care about them, then we will spend time alone with each of them as well as in the group. Time spent with a wife or a husband or a child or friend in the presence of others (even other members of the family) does not have the same value as time alone with the person to whom we wish to show our love. We often deny those whom we love the time which is necessary for a genuine communication and expression of caring. Relationship can seldom, if ever, be given in a pill or a gift.

This was brought out to me in a very dramatic manner some years ago. Returning home after a hard day's work, I had to make two calls at the hospital before dinner. My seventeen-year-old daughter asked me if she might drive me there. I should have suspected that she had something on her mind, for she hated to drive. I remember clearly that we were turning left from Mountain Avenue to Royal Oaks, when she exploded a quiet bomb, saying: "Father, when are you going to treat my mother like a human being?" I was dumbstruck. She had the courage to point out to me the obvious fact that my busyness had prevented me from seeing.

Later that evening my wife and I sat down to talk. I realized that I had become so busy that we seldom ever had prime time together in which to relate. I had begun to take her for granted. We seldom ever had time alone. I proposed that we turn over a new leaf. I would take her out for dinner at least once a week. We would have a good meal and a glass of wine, and we would talk. During the following twenty years we have visited many good restaurants. The pleasant time together has renewed and revitalized our marriage. *Love cannot be expressed without making time for the person whom we would love.*

I found that the same practice worked with my children. If I had come to my son or daughter and said: "Now we have time together and we are going to talk," the steel doors would have clanged shut. If, however, I asked one of them to go to dinner with me, then the stage was set and communication could flow. I also discovered that over the years my children's taste in restaurants improved.

I have found that once the doors are opened, then I

must be as available to them as I am to any client or parishioner who wants to talk. How jealous my children were of those who came to talk to me! They wanted some of my time, too. Spending time with each member of the family makes it possible for each one of them to ask for time when they need it. Susanna Wesley, the mother of John and Charles and the other creative Wesleys, had twenty children. She made a rule to spend at least one hour alone with each one of them each week. The effect of such caring is incalculable. Of course, when we have finally heard those we love, we need to act upon the data we have received or we simply reinforce the idea that we do not care.

I discovered that each of my children needed time alone with me several times a month if I was to stay in real relationship with them. I have discovered that as they grow older and become adults, they need and deserve my time as much as when they were children. We seldom set aside this kind of time until we realize how important it is and give it priority.

The Power of Positive Feedback

If we want to express love to those within the family circle, we will also stand up for them when they are subjected to condemnation or criticism from the world or from themselves. Our acceptance and praise are much more likely to give strength, direction, and solid morality than picky judgment and continued harping about what is wrong. Few things bothered me more as a child than being told how bad or stupid or wrong I was when I already knew that and suffered from the guilt of it. I needed help to overcome the problems, not to be driven further into the mire. I needed understanding, not added criticism.

Parents often make the mistake of thinking that they must produce fine, perfect children solely by their direction and discipline. Of course the things which bother us most in our children are the very aspects of our own lives that we have not been able to handle or of which we are afraid. These things may not be our children's problems.

The task of parenting is to provide an atmosphere in which the spiritual, loving forces in the child may be recognized and mobilized. This is not possible when we still unconsciously look at children as little monsters who must be whipped into shape. Love provides better limits and growth patterns than rigid rules and unbending justice about them. Positive feedback usually creates more change for good than criticism. This is true in the classroom as well as the family. Most of us want to grow and please. Please remember, however, that I am not saying that love does not set limits and enforce them.

Many years ago I visited two social workers who shared with me the story of two separate pairs of children they adopted. They tried to raise the first pair of children with total objectivity, as was popular fifty years ago. Within a year they had to return these children to the orphanage, as they had become incorrigible. The couple did not give up. They took two more children into their home from the same orphanage. This time, however, the home was to be the children's fortress. They showered them with love and stood up for them when they were in trouble with neighbors or in school. These children thrived, stayed with them, and went on to college. They realized the truth of Van der Post's statement: "One cannot just pick out what one likes in people and reject the rest. That's using people, not loving them."[4]

Everyone of us needs a place where we are accepted and considered valuable whether we are right or wrong. A real friend or parent or spouse is one who is behind us whether we are right or wrong, just because they are with us and love us. St. Monica stood by Augustine in this way as he passed through the sewers of the ancient world. My friend Starr Daily experienced this kind of love when his father stood by him, caring, not judging, for his twenty years in and out of prison. Finally the message got through, and Starr was transformed. My experience is that I seldom help others by judging them; I merely add to the burden of guilt they are already carrying. Most of us carry more guilt than others realize. Ian McClaren knew what he was talking about when he wrote: "Be kind; for everyone is carrying a heavy burden."

The opposite of judgment and criticism is looking for potential in the other person, dwelling on the positive and creative rather than upon the negative. Looking for potential and hoping for its expression often actualizes it, as was shown in an experiment carried out in an elementary school. A group of teachers were given reports on the children whom they were going to teach. In these profiles the mental ability (IQ's) of the children was recorded at much higher levels than they had actually received when tested. At the end of the school year these children had achieved in accordance with what the teachers thought their abilities were, rather than what their actual intelligence quotients indicated they might attain.

As a child my parents feared that I was not as bright as they hoped. A brain injury at birth had disabled me and made it difficult for me to speak with clarity, and my manual dexterity was very poor. I did not do well in school until I met a fifth grade teacher who saw that I had potential, that I had an active imagination and liked to think. Suddenly the world changed and I began to come into my own. I discovered I could do very well in school. How deeply grateful I am to that teacher who allowed me to become what I might become! How many of us could reach to higher levels of achievement and capacity if someone took the trouble to treat us this way? B. F. Skinner has demonstrated the effectiveness of operant conditioning (rewards for performance). When this technique is coupled with genuine love, miracles occur.

Few of us grow to our potential unless we are loved. Love not only sees potential, it helps it come to being. In his novel *The Face Beside the Fire* Van der Post describes this capacity of love in these telling words:

If there is one telling image inherited from the past that causes much fatal, cynical and ironical misunderstanding, it is the image of the blindness of love. If there is one thing love is not, it is blind.

106

If it possesses a blindness at all, it is a blindness to the man and the man-made blindnesses of life; to the dead-ends, the cul-de-sacs and hopelessnesses of our being. In all else it is clear and far-sighted as the sun. When the world and judgment say: "This is the end," love alone can see the way out. It is the aboriginal tracker, the African bushman on the faded desert spoor within us, and its unfailing quarry is always the light.[5]

It is impossible to love those around us if we do not know something about how human beings function, how they respond, about their nature and structure. No one would think of applying for a job as an accountant who knew nothing about numbers. No one would try to be a farmer without some experience in planting and harvesting. No one would try to be a doctor without training and experience. And yet most of us try to relate to our children, our friends, our spouses, without ever learning the well-established facts discovered by psychologists over the past eighty years. Love needs knowledge if it is to function responsibly. Everyone has a psychology, a view of what we human beings are like and how we function. Some of the popular views about human nature are woefully inadequate. We need to stop and see what our psychology is. If we don't, we are likely to accept one that is inadequate, an inferior one which holds us in its clutches because it is never questioned. In a later chapter we shall deal with the knowledge we need to have if we are going to be able to love intelligently and maturely.

Hostility and Love

This brings us to the subject of the hostilities which all of us feel at one time or another in our intimate relationships. Sooner or later those close to us will step on our toes. If we refuse to admit to ourselves that we have any anger and hostility, we often push it down into the unconscious, pretending that it is not there. There it festers, grows and erupts, often in totally inappropriate places. Or else we move away from those who have hurt us and our relationship can grow colder and colder until it finally dies.

David Augsburger has written a fine study of hostility and what to do with it in a book, *Anger and Assertiveness in Pastoral Counseling.* What he says applies to all of us, not just pastoral counselors. He shows how the good-guy syndrome separates people, makes relationships unreal and is often one aspect of fear and hostility rather than genuine goodness. How can we deal with these hostilities within us?

I was invited to come to the Church of the Savior in Washington, D.C., to speak on this very subject. Few churches are more consciously Christian. Those who attended discovered as they tried to come together in real fellowship that anger and hostility and conflict were often released. As I reflected with these people we realized that there were some creative ways to handle hostility.

First of all I need to catch my anger while it is still in flight, before it has come down upon another person. This requires that I am aware of my own hostile potential and that I am able to pause between feeling and action. Angry impulses need to be looked at before they are expressed. This takes some doing and requires a degree of consciousness and a determination to learn control of my emotions.

Then as I reflect I have to ask myself some questions: Is my angry reaction appropriate to the situation or is it out of context with what has happened? Am I truly upset because of this event or am I using this event to let out accumulated frustration and anger which I have not dealt with before? *Most often I discover that I can control my anger when the person is one who can harm me and I let it out when I am in a power position, when those around me cannot hurt me.* I discovered that in the past I had often bottled up my anger toward people in the parish so that butter would not melt in my mouth and then discharged this anger at home upon my wife and children. That kind of anger is unfair, unloving and un-Christian.

If I am in communication with those around me, I can listen to them when I have expressed anger. I need to listen to them when they tell me that my expression of aggression and anger is out of bounds and inappropriate. Then I can begin to look into myself and try to find the source of my anger and hurt and deal with them.

When I have exploded in anger in an inappropriate way I can always apologize. This does not always undo all the damage, but it heals some of the hurt which I have caused. When we cannot admit that we are out of line and ask for forgiveness, we simply destroy intimate closeness.

When I catch my anger before it alights I can change my angry statement from an accusation or judgment into a statement of my own feeling. It is one thing to be called stupid and uncaring; it is quite another to have our child or friend say: "What you have done has upset me and caused me to feel uncared for and unimportant." The simple transposition of negative, attacking statements into statements of feeling goes a long way in handling hostilities among those who are close to us. My wife and I have worked for thirty-seven years to keep loving one another. Statements of feeling rather than attack have helped us enormously. This suggestion sounds very simple, but it is incredibly effective. Saying that I feel that you are being unfair is different from calling you a liar.

There is a school of marriage counseling which teaches what it calls fair fighting. Along with the well-known marriage therapist Luciano L'Abate, I believe that fair fighting seldom achieves intimacy. It may produce a working cold war, but in order to achieve a real, caring, tender relationship we need to look beneath our hostilities. Behind nearly every anger is a hurt, a pain or an injury. Real intimacy involves sharing hurt feelings.[6]

Although sexuality is important in marriage relationships, problems of sexual relationship do not produce the greatest number of marriage conflicts and divorces. Problems relating to money have this dubious honor; hostility generated because two people cannot come to an agreement as to a fair distribution of their income breaks up more homes than anything else. Where people can share feelings and relate openly as equals, this kind of hostility is largely eliminated.

One of the reasons that we find it difficult to relate is

that we have hidden expectations of one another. Until these are brought out into the open and discussed, there will be guerrilla warfare. What are my hidden expectations of my wife and what are hers of me? The hidden nature of such expectations was illustrated in one of my classes. We were talking about our hidden agendas and a very lovely young woman who had been in a convent for seven years spoke up and said: "Oh, but I have no expectations. I can give, expecting nothing in return." I asked her what her feelings would be in the following situation. She has a friend who is very sick in the hospital, and she visits her every day for several weeks. Finally the friend gets well. Then she gets sick herself, and the friend whom she had visited comes into the hospital but does not stop in to see her. What would be her response? She replied, a little taken aback: "Why, I would be hurt or maybe even a bit angry. I would have expected her to stop."

This is a very human reaction, but it is not the stuff of which Christian love is made. If I am visiting you in the hospital, I do it because I love you and not because I expect anything back. For this reason visiting the dying is often an expression of pure charity and love. And if I am in the hospital and one is passing by whom I have visited, I hope that I can love that person enough to let him or her pass by. When I do something for another person, not because I want to give but because of hidden expectations of receiving something in return, this is not love, but a type of emotional barter. The phrase in the prayer of St. Francis is important for this very reason: "Divine Master, grant that I may not seek so much to be loved as to love."

And this brings us to the complexity of our motives. Seldom do I ever have pure motives. If we think that we must have pure motives before we can act in love, we will never act. There are all sorts of nasty, self-seeking voices within me. What I need to do in most situations is search out my primary motives. If they are all right, then I can act without fear.

This became abundantly clear to me in one situation. I was asked to be of help to a disturbed young man in an important and powerful family. I did what I could and helped the individual through a crisis. Instead of thanks I received hostility and some backbiting from the parents. Later I was talking to my friend Hilde Kirsch about how badly I had been treated, and she replied to me, "Well, Morton, did you give of yourself in order to get something back? Now you know what it means to be one of God's chosen people."

In another situation I was worried because I was spending a lot of time with a person in trouble whose family could do a lot for me. I was well aware of that, but I also realized that I would have done just as much for that person even if he had no connections and could give me nothing in return. Then I was free to pour my love and concern out without guilt or fear that I was doing the wrong thing.

There are some levels of hostility within me which I cannot let out on those around me without releasing destructiveness. Each of us has our murderer within, the raging, tormented one within who can cut up and destroy whatever it meets. In his autobiography, *Report to Greco*, the Greek writer Nikos Kazantzakis writes eloquently of how he discovered this barbaric level within himself. As he was walking with a friend one moonlit night, he saw the lights of the village gleaming below. "At that point an astonishing thing happened to me. I still shudder when I recall it. Halting, I shook my clenched fist at the village and shouted in a furor, 'I shall slaughter you all!'" The voice was not even his own. He had discovered that "inside us there is layer upon layer of darkness—raucous voices, hairy hungering beasts."[7]

And how do we deal with this? It certainly cannot be let out indiscriminately, or it will destroy. Instead we can bring this level of ourselves to God, the Risen Christ, who had dealt with and conquered this level of darkness. Sometimes it is helpful to share this level with a trusted friend, spiritual director or psychotherapist. The right people can help us carry this dark destructiveness, particularly if they know their own inner beast; however, I have found that only Christ can transform that darkness and lift it from us.

111

In *The Other Side of Silence* I have given some examples of bringing this level of myself to the Risen Christ.

Loving the Aged

In civilizations where family life has not broken down, the aged and elderly are usually given a place of honor and importance. We see this in China, in Japan, and in many other cultures. The same attitude was found in Western Europe before materialism made its inroads and the nuclear family made the elderly not only obsolete, but a nuisance. In most developed civilizations the wisdom and experience of the aged have been admired, and the deceased are remembered in much the same way that the elderly are honored. They are not forgotten because they are dead.

There are few more tragic places than many of the nursing homes in which so great a number of the aged are placed as soon as they cannot take care of themselves, and sometimes even before. We seem to want them out of the way. I wonder if we have truly come to understand what love is within the family and among friends until we have a high place for parents and grandparents and go out to show them love whether they seem conscious of what we are bringing or not. I have discussed the subject of visiting the dying in *Afterlife: The Other Side of Dying.*

I wonder if we can truly love other people if we see their lives ending with the grave. It is my firm conviction that life does go on and that we are not entirely cut off from those who have died. This is the meaning of the phrase "the Communion of the Saints" in the Apostles' Creed. Dr. McCauley, a psychiatrist in Great Britain, has discovered evidence which suggests that we are more tied to our family dead than we might believe. He has found that it is helpful to remember those who have had a special place in our lives at Eucharist and at other times. If we have truly loved and if the dead continue on, it is not love to wash our hands of them once they have died. In most Eucharistic services we pray for the deceased as well as the living.

Love to the aged needs to be expressed in concrete actions of concern. When it is, amazing things happen. A friend shared the following letter with me. His brother, an Army colonel, wrote telling of reaching out to his mother in a nursing home:

I went last Tuesday to see Mother. As it is almost Christmas, I wanted to drop off a few trifling but ornately wrapped presents for her so that she would have more to look forward to as the holidays approached. Mother was in her room waiting for me—it was still morning; we talked for a while; there were silences. One sometimes does not know how to fill conversational gaps after the amenities and conversation pieces are laid to rest.

Mother offered me a banana which I accepted, peeled and ate. I got her fur hat down from the top shelf so she could wear it to church during winter. There were again the silences of a thousand unspoken things. I asked her how the food was; she said it was terrible. I weighed in my mind if this was the normal barracks room disdain for all things that cooks do or was it for real.

Lunch time came and we went down to the dining room. Mother introduced me again to a dozen people for the first time that I had met many times before. The priest said grace. We had moussaka—it was a Greek Orthodox home—it was quite good. The administrator of the home announced that at 1:30 a woman's club from nearby New Jersey was coming to visit the home and sponsor a party. The priest said grace again.

We went down to the recreation room to see the Christmas tree that Christina, one of the girls who works at the home, had decorated. It was about five feet tall, ample in girth and tastefully decorated. We sat on the couch and talked a while. I addressed some Christmas cards to some of Mother's relatives and friends. It was almost 1:30. I thought of leaving so as to avoid the party, but I stayed.

The club women came in with smiles, gifts

and pastries. Their priest was with them, a fine looking man with an easy, no-nonsense manner. The guests sat at a long table; there were about thirty of them. The residents sat at smaller tables. Mother and I shared a table with two other ladies. I was wondering if I could make a graceful exit at this point.

Christina then acted as the mistress of ceremonies; she called on Caliope, one of the residents, who recited some poetry. She did a nice job and got some applause. Next, one of the male residents sang several songs in a strong, impassioned voice. One of the younger women from the guest table ran over and kissed him, with much applause.

Christina then said that she would like to have one of the residents give her impression of the home for the benefit of the guests, as this was the first time that this particular club had come to St. Michael's Home. She asked Mother if she would do this. Mother gave an impromptu talk describing a typical day at the home; she told of the daily routines, the various services available and the usual activities in a clear and forthright manner. When she was finished she launched into a talk about why it was right that she should be there, and that old people should not harass their children; she went on to describe old age. She said old people were like the mountains in the winter, snow on top, their moons—eyes—were dimmed, their millstones—teeth—grinding exceedingly poorly and that she now had three legs. Several ladies at the long, narrow guest table were openly wiping their eyes. At this point, something unexpected happened that I shall never forget. Mother broke into a song that I had never heard before. The words were unimportant; the song had a strange springy, nostalgic lilt to it—out of this little white-haired old lady a vibrant, powerful aura was emitted. As she sang you saw tall mountains, deep ravines, rushing streams, dew-fresh mountain flowers—all from the eyes of a young girl, you heard of eternal hope and of promises yet unfulfilled, of brave un-educated people, of free spirits leaving their sacred soil for a remote new world, of the will to conquer any obstacles, and that men and women should prevail. You heard the sadness of a life inexorably approaching its end yet achieving hope through one's children—continuing tears from an increasing number of people—tears were in my eyes, too.

Afterwards many people came to talk to Mother, kiss her or take her hand. Their understanding and compassion showed; the guests soon left. Mother and I went to her room. It was around 4 o'clock. I said my goodbyes and left, pressing hands with all of those small gray figures who stopped me in the hallway and asked me to come back soon.

A Humbling Personal Lesson in Loving

My second son had not yet learned to read during fifth grade. After considering all the possibilities we finally settled on a remedial school. Our son had asked to go to a private school but disliked the one we chose for him. It was an excellent school, and the first thing they did was to administer a battery of psychological tests to him. And then I found myself in the unusual position of being on the other side of the table with the psychologist asking me, "Do you have any idea what this child's problem is?" I replied that I didn't know of any reason other than stubbornness and obstinacy. And then he dropped the bombshell: "The problem with this child is that he doesn't think that you really care for him or love him."

I protested vigorously that whenever I tried to show him love, warmth and affection, he pushed me away. The psychologist continued, "Has it ever occurred to you why he pushes you away? He is testing you to see how much you really do love him."

"At eleven years of age?" I asked.

115

"Even at eleven."

I decided on the spot that I was going to love that child if it killed me. And it did kill part of me. We went horseback riding together. Even though I have the manual dexterity of a palsied hippopotamus, I tried to do woodworking with him and other manual activities which he enjoyed. The real turnaround, however, came one day in a motel on the ocean front at Laguna Beach. I came into his room one morning and asked: "Johnnie, wouldn't you like to go swimming with me?"

Then, as only an eleven-year-old can say it, he replied, "Nah . . . I'd rather watch television."

In the past when I got this kind of response I would leave feeling rejected to spend my time doing something I would have preferred doing anyway. But after the psychologist's revelation I thought to myself, "Perhaps he is only testing me; I'll keep my sense of humor and pursue him." In a very playful manner (and this playful attitude was most important) I capered over to the TV set and turned it off. We tussled around the room, out the door, down the stairs, around the corner, out on the walkway and down into the ocean.

Do you know what that child said as we emerged from the first wave? He blew the water from his nose and exclaimed, "Father, I wondered how long it would take you to do this."

The old pattern was broken and we began to relate. His Iowa tests went up three years in six months' time. He began to learn to read. But don't think that this was the end of the struggle. One day as we were sitting beside a pool in Arizona where he was living (he was nineteen at the time), he spoke to me calmly and deliberately: "Father, you know, I have never liked you very well." This was not what my bruised ego needed at that moment, but I remembered I was going to try to show love. I remembered what the headmaster of a school told parents to do when their children said that they did not like them. I replied, "John, I don't blame you; there are many times that I don't like me either."

From that moment things between us mutated to a

116

new level. A year or so later John was with me at a conference I was giving, and I decided to tell the story I have just related. I wanted to hear his response. On the way to the place where we were staying that night, John spoke up: "Father, did I actually say that?" I nodded an assent.

The next morning as we were breakfasting John initiated the conversation: "Father, I remember when I made up my mind that I would never ask you for anything again in my life." I asked him to tell me about it.

"I was seven years old. You had been reading A. Conan Doyle's *Tales of Sherlock Homes* to my brother and me." He could even remember the author and the book. "My brother was away for several days, but I wanted you to read aloud to me anyway, and so I brought you the book and asked you to read. You said that you were too busy. I brought the book the next night, and you said that you were too busy. The same thing happened on the third night, and quite consciously I made up my mind that I would never ask *you* for anything else again in my life."

I had not realized how sensitive and needing of my love and attention this son of mine was. My refusal to read had struck at him as effectively as if I had wielded a club. I, of course, did not even remember the incident. However, patient love can even restore the years which the locusts have eaten, and a deep and real relationship has finally developed between us. In a recent family crisis which could have been serious but wasn't, John stuck by me and ministered to me with more love, sensitivity and concern than I have felt from the finest of psychotherapists.

7

Love, Sex and Christianity

We cannot deal with love without dealing with sex and sexuality. We cannot deal with sex without dealing with love, although there are some who try. The recent report of a commission of Roman Catholic theologians, *Human Sexuality*, tries to do just that and falls into total absurdity and unreality. This book corrects many false impressions, but the essential connection between love and sexuality is avoided like the serpent in the Garden of Eden.

It may appear audacious or silly to deal with the complex subject of sexuality and love in the few pages which we can allot to the subject in this book, but not to do so would be a cop-out; it would be avoiding a central aspect of love. Hundreds of books and thousands of novels have been written on the subject of human sexual attraction. Objective, scientific studies of how human beings function sexually have only been available for a little over ten years. The studies of Masters and Johnson are not the final word about sex, but they provide the most comprehensive hard data on the subject and must be taken into account in any serious discussion of the subject.

As briefly as possible we shall first of all discuss the strange devaluation of sex which is found in most conventional Christianity. After we have examined the roots from which this rejection of sexuality stems, we shall move on to the various levels of sexual expression. We shall then look at the essential difference between falling in love and loving, and conclude with some practical guidelines for dealing with this knotty, thorny and fascinating problem area of human existence.

Sexuality and Christianity

I remember clearly my first lesson in sex. I was about six years old and was walking downtown with my mother. So strongly did the lesson fix itself in my mind that I remember the very spot where I asked my mother why Aunt Gertrude, who was an unmarried school teacher, did not have any children. We were passing by the church and it was right in front of the beautiful stained glass window that this question popped out of me. My mother was the daughter of a Presbyterian minister, and her mother was the daughter of a Presbyterian minister. Puritanism was in our blood. She stopped, speechless, coughed, turned red and said something which I don't remember. But I got the message. This was an untouchable, dangerous, evil and ugly subject. The subject never came up again until I was about to go off to college and my father brought the subject up with such embarrassment that I relieved him of the necessity of discussing it by saying I was already informed.

I have listened to thousands of people discuss their sexual problems in the last thirty-five years, and I find that my experience, far from being unique, was run-of-the-mill. One finds it among nearly all people over forty and even among many of the "liberated" younger generation. This view of sexuality as dangerous, dark and evil is axiomatic to most Protestants; within many religious orders in the Catholic Church and through celibate teachers in parochial schools this same unconscious attitude is passed on from generation to generation. One even finds this same horror among atheists and agnostics who think that they have broken away from all religious belief. The problem is that this attitude is so hidden that it is seldom consciously professed, and so there is nothing to rebel against. It is very difficult to disengage ourselves from unconscious assumptions.

And most people think that this attitude is the official and only view of Christianity. Nothing could be further from the truth. If we will carefully read the entire Bible and every word of Christ, we find little in the Old Testament even suggesting this view of sexuality. Only one statement of Christ's could possibly be viewed in this light, and that is his statement about making ourselves eunuchs for the kingdom of God. Yet few people take Jesus' statement to the rich, young ruler about getting rid of all wealth as applying to everyone. This suggestion about sexuality was also probably given to a specific person with a specific problem.

When we study the Bible we discover that it contains five quite different views about sex.[1] We find in the Old Testament three varying outlooks: the glorification of sexuality in the Song of Songs, the naturalness of sexuality in the Book of Ruth, and the necessity to keep sexuality directed toward childbearing in much of the legal code of the Torah (the Books of the Law). The last of these views is understandable inasmuch as the Israelites were a small nation in the midst of hostile and warring opponents. The New Testament provides us with the attitude of Jesus toward family life and children. Even though Jesus was never married, he seemed to continue the very human and natural view of sexuality of most of the Old Testament. In St. Paul we begin to find a less propitious view of sexual relationships, but his thinking was colored by a belief that the end of the world was near. He believed that it was unfair to bring children into those troubled times and that people needed to direct their attention toward preparing for the end of the age.

Some centuries later when St. Ambrose was advising celibacy for women, there was no suggestion that one should avoid marriage because sexuality is evil. The reason was that in that society women often became either the slaves or the playthings of their husbands and were unable to follow the Christian way. The utter rejection of sex was first expressed by some monks living in the desert (an attitude still found on Mount Athos where not even chickens, because they are female, are allowed to soil the holy ground). It is, however, through St. Augustine that this view passed into popular Christian thought and practice.

St. Augustine was a great thinker in many ways, but his views on sexuality were colored by his own personal life and by the teachings of the Manichean sect which he followed for nine years during his youth and early adulthood. Augustine was brought up a Christian, but he reacted against his family's Christianity and entered the sewers of the ancient world. He had a mistress and an illegitimate son whom he abandoned (!) when he was converted. Apparently he went into a reaction formation when he left his former way of life. The Manicheans were a gnostic sect believing that the physical world was the creation of an evil God, opposed to the spiritual, good God, and that the body and everything about it, sex in particular, was evil. Even though one of the most important struggles of the Early Church Fathers was directed against this point of view, Augustine apparently never got it out of his system.

Augustine's treatise, *The Good of Marriage*, has to be read in order to be believed. Although marriage is good, sexuality which is not for the express purpose of conceiving children is a venial sin; and even sexual intercourse for that purpose is an inferior state to virginity. Augustine writes that married couples "are better in proportion as they begin earlier to refrain by mutual consent from sexual intercourse." Later he writes that "in marriage, intercourse for the purpose of generation has no fault attached to it, but for the purpose of satisfying concupiscence, provided [even] with a spouse, because of the marriage fidelity, it is a venial sin; adultery or fornication, however, is a mortal sin." One student of Augustine has written that among all the bodily appetites only sexual desire seemed to Augustine to be irreconcilable with human rationality and decency. We find this attitude scattered through Augustine's writings. One is hard put to find where in the teachings of Jesus Augustine could support such a point of view.[2]

The basic gnostic myth which underlies this kind of

121

thinking is a simple one. I have discussed it in several other places, but since it is critical to an understanding of Augustine and much of the Christian attitude which springs from him, I will repeat it here. According to the gnostic creation story, creation was a tragedy. Once upon a time all spiritual reality was gathered together in one vast pleroma, a spiritual pool of ecstatic bliss. And somehow a catastrophe occurred; an explosion took place within this spiritual body and bits and fragments of this spiritual substance were flung out from their spiritual home. Some even fell so far as to come in contact with formless, chaotic, recalcitrant, earthy, evil matter. Where this conjunction occurred a monstrosity was formed, the human being which was part evil matter and part pure spirit.

Ultimately our theory of salvation depends upon the myth which describes the origin and nature of the universe. Thus according to gnostic theory we are saved as we separate our spiritual selves out from entangling and corrupting physical bodies and desires. To do this we need knowledge (gnosticism comes from the Greek word for knowledge) which shows us the way of salvation and directs us on a path of asceticism that gradually detaches us from matter and physicality. There is, however, something worse than failing to follow the way of knowledge and ascetic practices. Bringing new life into this evil physical existence is the primal sin. Conception is totally evil. Sexuality is closely tied to conception and so shares in the ugly awfulness of this irredeemable physical world. Even though the church has expressly denied that conception and sexuality are evil in themselves, its actions and statements (even those of some of the acknowledged saints) seem to support such a conclusion.

Whenever the material world is seen as truly evil, then the body will appear evil and sexuality will also be tainted with evil. All pleasure connected with the body and the world also appears evil. This is certainly not the attitude of the Old Testament which tells us that God created the world and it was good; it is not the view of Jesus of Nazareth who saw the beauty and innocence of children and

122

families and who changed water into wine at the marriage of Cana.

The Varieties of Sexual Expression

One of the main problems in talking about sexuality is that the value of sexuality depends not so much upon the act itself as it does upon the circumstances in which the act is performed. Sex, like making money, can be a valuable or destructive thing. One person makes money in order to make slaves of people and build up his or her own power; another does it to provide jobs for needy people. Sexuality can be an expression of any of the following conditions:

1. It can be the expression of two committed people for whom this physical union is the ultimate, ecstatic sacramental expression of the love which they bear toward one another. For some people, such an experience may be a window into heaven.

2. It can also be a really blissful expression of two people meeting and merging for the moment. Van der Post writes of such an experience in *The Seed and the Sower.* However, this experience, unless it is continued in a permanent relationship, fails to come to its fullest fruition, as Masters and Johnson show so clearly in *The Pleasure Bond.* They maintain that genuine sexual joy grows only to the extent that two people learn to communicate in depth with each other. Sexual satisfaction is as much psychological as physical.

3. Sexual life may be a duty which one or both partners give to the other in spite of their fears and hangups about sex. Such people miss much of the joy in life and much of the meaning of love.

4. Sexuality can be the attempt to find pleasure or physical release in a casual, sexual encounter. If sexuality is a sacrament of love, this is prostitution of sex whether the pleasure is freely given or paid for.

5. One person with power over another can seduce another into the sex act by either sexual attractiveness, or psychological persuasion, or control over the other's life. When

sexual intercourse is forced on another by my power just for pleasure, I am using the other person just as much as if I were an owner of slaves. Prostitution is slavery with a time limit.

6. Sex can be a brutal act of aggression and violence. Rape is nearly always a devastating, demoralizing and traumatic experience.

Sex and sexual expression can be on the one hand an outward and visible sign of human and divine love. On the other it can be one of the most brutal and dehumanizing actions with which we victimize another person. Unfortunately much of the church since Augustine has failed to speak of the sacramental aspect of sexuality.

One often wonders what is the purpose of this mysterious power of sexuality which can be so abused. In his excellent book *Marriage: Dead or Alive*, Adolf Guggenbuhl-Craig asks this very question. He comes to the conclusion that the ultimate purpose of sexuality is to goad us on to wholeness and integration, to God himself. It has a far greater value than just the reproduction of the race, at least in the human species.

When Is Our Action Really Sexual?

And when does our action become sexual? Is sexuality restricted to the actual stimulation of the sex organs or to intercourse, or is it our total human response to each other which sometimes results in the sex act? This is a thorny question and the answer depends to a certain extent on how we use and define our words. Let's look at various levels of sexual expression.

1. Probably no one would deny that actual genital intercourse is sexual. However, is it full sexuality when one of the partners is seduced or forced into the relationship or if the sex act is merely duty in order to produce children?

2. Are we being fully sexual when our action involves the stimulation of the sex organs without intercourse between either man and woman or two of the same sex, or by oneself? Are we being sexual if there is no orgasm?

124

3. Then there is the whole area of expressions of human closeness—hugging, kissing, touching the skin . . . This may involve genital stimulation or not. When people are uninhibited such actions certainly can lead to a full expression of genital sexuality.

4. Even the simple holding of another's hand can convey sexuality in a powerful manner. One nun told me about a certain brother in a religious order who held her hand; she felt something other than brotherly love in this touch. In another instance a counselee of mine was having an affair with his secretary and the only place they could meet without discovery was at church. He told me that sitting next to her in church was an intense sexual experience for him.

5. And then there is the desire for physical closeness. Often it is combined with a fantasy about further closeness. Jesus speaks about those who commit adultery in their hearts.

I would conclude that we are most likely to be sexual beings if we are alive at all. Except for a few anchorites, human beings have a deep need for closeness. Love without some tinge of this desire for closeness is likely to be the "glassy Christian love" of which Berdyaev wrote in *The Meaning of the Creative Act.* I don't want anyone to be kind and "love" me merely out of duty. In spite of all that is written theologically about the difference between *eros* (the love which desires and seeks the other for ourselves) and *agape* (the love which is purely centered in the other person), I doubt very much that they can be neatly divided in spite of what the Swedish theologian Nygren writes. If agape doesn't have some touch of eros, it is forbidding and cold. If eros doesn't have a dash of agape, it is not love at all, but pure possessiveness.

Eros and *agape* are different poles of the same reality; they are not entirely different aspects of life. When we have listened to hundreds of people and reflected deeply on our own lives, I doubt if we can come to any other conclusion.

What Is Falling in Love?

Only with the advent of depth psychology has there appeared an adequate explanation of the process of falling in love. It is truly astounding that an emotional state so common and important to the human race should have been shrouded in mystery so long.

Depth psychology has come to three basic conclusions about human beings which relate to this powerful experience of being in love.

1. All of us human beings have an unconscious aspect of our personalities, part of our psychological being of which we are unconscious at most times.

2. In each of us, both in our bodies and our psyches, there are evidences of both masculine and feminine qualities. Males have vestigial breasts and female hormones; women's bodies contain physical remnants of male sexuality. The same bisexuality applies to our psyches. Most men have feminine psychic elements in the depth of their unconscious, and women have masculine qualities.

3. One of the deepest desires of human beings, one of the strongest instincts (the primary pre-conscious urges), is to bridge the split between conscious and unconscious, to be whole, unitary, one, in touch with all of one's self, both masculine and feminine.

Falling in love is an outer, almost sacramental, way of achieving this desired wholeness. Let's illustrate it in a diagram:

conscious Man ⟵⟶ conscious Woman
━━━━━━━━━━━━━━   ━━━━━━━━━━━━━━
unconscious ⟋⟍ unconscious masculine
feminine qualities   qualities

This pictures the inner woman (feminine qualities) in each man and the inner man (masculine qualities) within each woman. When we fall in love we suddenly see our inner feminine in some woman or our inner masculine in some man. The arrows represent our capacity to project on others. We may even discover our inner contrasexual part for the first time by projecting it out upon a person of the opposite sex. When this happens we have fallen in love. We desire to be close to the other, to join in a psychological and physical union with him or her. In this way we are achieving a kind of ersatz union with ourselves. I asked the counselee who met his beloved in church what he got from the experience. He answered with these revealing words: "When I am sitting next to her, I feel whole."

All projection is not evil. The projection process actually enables us to discover parts of ourselves lost in the unconscious which we might not otherwise recognize as part of us. Also, projection can help us bridge the enormous gap which usually exists between two people. It brings two of us together so we can begin a relationship. The projection of our inner feminine or masculine sides (our ideal woman or man) is evil only when we truly believe that this ecstatic initiating state is the norm in human relationships. As we begin to live with another person, we usually discover that the other person is quite different from the ideal person we have projected upon him or her. Ideal people do not exist. When the ecstatic projection falls off, then a *real* relationship can begin between two people.

When we come to the disillusioning realization that the beloved is different than we thought or wanted, we can do one of two things. We can call off the relationship and, if we have been married in the process, get a divorce; most multiple marriages are the result of failing to realize the difference between the inner image which we project on other people and reality. Instead of working out the nitty-gritty of human interactions, people go on looking for the illusory idea. *Or we can get about the business of knowing ourselves and the other person in reality and of starting to truly love each other.* This is indeed a challenge which can last throughout life. Madeleine L'Engle has written profoundly about her personal marriage challenge in *The Irrational Season.*

The picture which we have presented of falling in love is, of course, oversimplified. Along with the lost or unknown masculine or feminine component of ourselves we may also project upon another person the image of the "holy," the beautiful, the self-sacrificial lover, the knight in shining armor, the all-caring parent, the damsel in distress or a thousand other variations. These other images can add and merge with our basic projection and greatly increase its power. A love affair can take on the quality of a religious experience. John Sanford has dealt with the whole subject of projection in human relationships in a thorough and creative way in his book *Our Invisible Partners.*

Guggenbuhl-Craig has pointed out more adequately than anyone else the "salvation" quality of a good marriage:

> A marriage only works if one opens himself to exactly that which he would never ask for otherwise. Only through rubbing oneself sore and losing oneself is one able to learn about oneself, God, and the world. Like every soteriological pathway, that of marriage is hard and painful.
>
> A writer who creates meaningful works does not want to become happy, he wants to be creative. Likewise married people can seldom enjoy happy, harmonious marriages, as psychologists would force upon them and lead them to believe. The image of the "happy marriage" causes great damage.
>
> For those who are gifted for the soteriological pathway of marriage, it, like every such pathway, naturally offers not only trouble, work, and suffering, but the deepest kind of existential satisfaction. Dante did not get to Heaven without traversing Hell. And so also there seldom exist "happy marriages."[3]

Sexuality is really as much psychological as physical. It can become the very glue which holds people together as they are working at their many differences in value and temperament. Falling in love which does not move toward creative loving such as we have described in the previous chapter usually ends in the breakup of a relationship, divorce or the hell of marital cold war.[4] Sexuality in a marriage which has moved toward true loving can be a sacramental expression of love which can even give an understanding of the incredible love of God.

Guidelines for Handling Our Capacity To Love

Fortunately or unfortunately as the case may be, human beings are not naturally monogamous as are some birds and animals. Some people can love an extraordinary number of other human beings. Within our society this can lead to tension, conflict, pain and tragedy. Here are some suggestions for dealing with this complex and universal problem. The only way to avoid this conflict entirely is to cease to love entirely, and this often results in drying up and blowing away.

1. Sexuality is not evil; it is part of being human. Healthy souls usually require healthy bodies. Rejection and devaluation of the body often ends in sickness and death. Alexander Lowen says it well:

> To know who one is, an individual must be aware of what he feels. He should know the expression on his face, how he holds himself, and the way he moves. Without this awareness of bodily feeling and attitude, a person becomes split into a disembodied spirit and a disenchanted body. . . . [5]

It is nearly impossible to love if we deny the value of the body and its feelings. If we balk at this statement, we probably need to reassess our whole value system.

2. The sexual problems of most committed couples are solvable. Holy sexuality is the result of trust, confidence, lack of fear and good communication. There are important things to learn from experts in sex therapy.[6]

3. One of the most harmful things that parents can do is to get sexually involved with their children. Incest nearly always involves traumatic tragedy. On the other hand, we need to have enough security and confidence to be able to speak to the sexual questions and fears which all people have as they are growing up. Two counselees of mine were talking with my thirty-year-old son and me about the sexual

taboos in their homes. My son spoke up and said: "Whenever I wanted to know something about sex I went to my father and asked him." This was almost unthinkable to the two counselees. A loving family in which there is genuine communication and trust can produce an atmosphere where such frankness is possible.

4. When we have sexual feelings we need to be honest with ourselves and with others and determine that we will *never* use another person. We must also quite consciously set our limits on what our sexual behavior is going to be. It is easier to get physically active than to talk about sexuality. Talking about sexuality often reduces the compulsiveness of sex.

5. Pastors, lawyers, doctors and others will be dealing one-to-one with many human beings. Such one-to-one encounters *nearly always* set the stage for transference (which is the technical name for falling in love in the psychotherapeutic community). The natural professional hazard of these vocations is seldom dealt with in their school training. Only the person who has some idea of the powerful forces existing in nearly any one-to-one encounter can possibly avoid them. Most people coming to the professional for one-to-one counseling have deeper needs than they realize. It is up to the *counselor* to set the *limits* in such matters and never exploit them. Touch stimulates transference. Avoidance of touch is helpful if we would avoid the acting out of transference.

6. Since most of us have some bisexual component, most of us can have these feelings for either sex. The best professional equipment to help one avoid the problems of transference is to know ourselves well through some apprenticeship with someone who has been through the war of intense relationships.

7. Sexuality which involves force or violence, either physical or psychological, is always dangerous and often demonic.

8. Whenever we are in a power position with another either in actuality or psychologically, we need to be very careful of any sexual expression and deeply conscious of our

motives in any sexual overture toward the one over whom we have that power.[7]

9. The idea that there is a completely safe method of birth control is an old wives' tale. Some of the brightest and most careful people I know have become pregnant or made others pregnant. There are more children born out of wedlock at the present than in former years. Children adopted out by parents who do not want them carry an incredibly difficult extra burden. Marriages contracted under the duress of pregnancy are more difficult than those where the choice is free. Terminated pregnancies involve considerable moral and psychological stress even among the most liberated people. Any actions which can result in pregnancy can trigger a time bomb. *The moral of all this is: be very careful of getting into any situation where a pregnancy may occur out of wedlock.*

10. Teenage sexuality poses real problems. There are good reasons for taboos on sexual activity among this age group. When young people indulge in sexual intercourse before they know what mature, loving relationships are, they split sexuality off from life and keep it from being the meaningful experience it can be later on. Sexual activity can short-circuit real relationship. Rollo May writes on this in *Love and Will*, and Kathleen Fury has written a provocative article, "Sex and the American Teenager," in the April 1980 issue of *Ladies' Home Journal.*

11. If we have an inordinate fear of sexuality and marriage, the solution is to get at the roots of the problem rather than opt for a celibate existence. There is an heroic vocation for genuine celibacy; it should not be degraded by those who take it on to avoid themselves.

12. Homosexuality has the same variety of integration with love as does heterosexuality. We should be careful that our judgment of homosexuality is not a projection of our own unconscious bisexuality. Fear of this aspect of our lives may cut us off from both sexes and make us incapable of relating to anyone.

13. Sexuality, as we have said earlier, is a very complex, confusing and difficult subject. Any of us who thinks that

we have our sexuality well under control should beware. We may be heading for a fall. No one who professes that the matter can easily be dealt with should be trusted.

14. We often need to find someone with whom we can talk over our sexual fears and doubts. As Freud showed abundantly, these fears and concerns can affect every area of life. It is difficult to find someone with whom to talk. One can look carefully for such a person, and one can pray about finding one. God's hand is not foreshortened, and he can still answer prayer and bring us the right listener. Those people who direct the spiritual lives of others need to be comfortable with and knowledgeable about sexuality if they are to help us in our spiritual journey. Sexuality and spirituality are much intertwined.

15. There are some excellent books which give important facts about sexuality and marriage. My wife and I have looked at many of them, and the one we have found which is least sexist and most complete is Nat Lehrman's *Masters and Johnson Explained* (New York, Playboy Press, 1979). What we do not know about is almost always frightening. We need to know the facts about sexuality. Old wives' tales are not adequate.

8

Learning About People
and How to Love Them

We human beings are certainly strange creatures. We
spend limitless time on unimportant things and little time
on some of the most crucial areas of our lives. We spend
twelve years in school learning to read and write and picking up enough math to balance our checkbooks and read
the financial pages of the newspaper. Some of us go on to
college to learn the fundamentals of a career or a profession. We can also spend hours and weeks and months learning how to play bridge or about dog breeding or baseball
averages. *However we seldom spend much time in learning
about other human beings and how we can get along with
them.* And yet our mental health, our happiness, and even
our life expectancy depend to a large degree on how well
we have learned about human beings and how to relate to
them.

We cannot love other human beings until we have
some idea what human beings are like and how we can interact with them. These reflections might well be considered an introductory chapter to a book which has not yet
been written on the fundamentals of a Christian psychology. As I have said before, if we do not have an adequate and

realistic psychology, we have an inadequate and erroneous one. I have not always felt that psychology was important. When I was first married (and I shudder to think of my action), I had my wife get rid of the psychology texts she had used in college. Like most people with this kind of attitude, I was very insecure, and I was afraid that psychology might find me out.

The suggestions I offer fall into three categories. First of all we need to realize the complexity of human personality and have some model, some picture of what human beings are like. Then we need to see that human beings are very different in the way they perceive, react and relate to the world around them. And last of all we will see that perfectly decent, well-intentioned human beings have very different value systems and different ideas about what is most important in human life.

First of all we need to realize that most of us do not know enough about the essential nature of human beings. Those who think that they already are adequately informed are probably as far behind the times as those farmers in third world countries who know nothing of crop rotation and fertilizer. And then we need to start some serious reading and study about human nature. However, we can read until our eyes grow dim, but we will find out little about our humanness until we begin to reflect on how we actually get along with our spouse, our children, the clerk at the store or our boss in light of what we have read. We humans are masters of self-deception and projection.

I had been many years in psychological analysis when I attended a group life laboratory. I had read a lot of books on psychology and I thought I knew myself quite well. However, the way that group responded to my attempts at manipulation showed me my arrogance and hostility in a way that changed my life. Everyone who would learn about human beings needs to find some experiential groups in which the nature of human beings is the central focus of study. My wife and I each taught courses at the University of Notre Dame having this orientation. Many of the students confided that those classes, which led them to reflect on the nature and response of human beings, were the most valuable they had taken in college.

What Makes Human Beings Tick?

Most of us have at one time or another been fascinated by a watch and have taken one apart in order to see what makes it work. If we were not so laden with assumptions and prejudices about human beings, we would find the study of our own species more interesting than any mechanism. We have already discussed the nature of human beings in Chapter 3. Let me now summarize what I have written and draw my diagram once again.

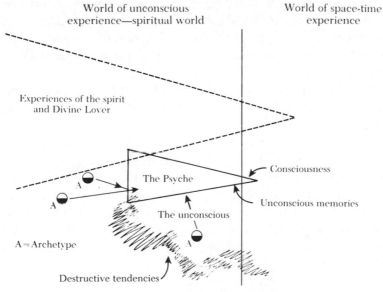

What can we observe from this diagram?

1. We have a human consciousness which usually reaches out into the world with five senses.

2. We have a rational capacity which takes this data and gradually produces a coherent picture of the world around us.

3. We are likely to be like a cork bobbing up and down on a wild ocean unless (a) we belong to and accept the ideas of a particular culture or group, or (b) we work out a consistent pattern of behavior. The first is given unconsciously by living in a particular culture. The second requires experience and discipline.

4. We are not exhausted by our rational consciousness. Our dreams, mistakes, fantasies, intuitions, visions, involuntary gestures, physical symptoms and mental quirks all remind us that there is something within us more than our rational, conscious mind and our sense experience. Although the word unconscious is a lousy one, it describes that part of our psyche of which we are not usually aware in our society. And yet that part determines a major portion of our lives. If we would have any influence on ourselves or other human beings, we need to be able to reach this unconscious level of them. *If we are truly to love others we must be able to understand this level of them and interact with it.*

5. Within this part of our psyches are forgotten memories of what we have experienced and vestigial remnants from the history of human development. *Through* this level of our being we are in touch with a vast realm of psychic reality akin to our own psyches but separate from it. An enormous realm of experience and data is available to us. It is as independent of us as the data of sense experience.

6. And on this level we come in contact with the inner idiot, the inner destroyer (the murderer within) and the very breath, hand and spirit of the Divine Lover, as well as a lot of other non-physical realities.

7. When we fail to realize that human beings are as complicated and multi-leveled as this, we are likely to treat them in an inadequate manner. Only through patient, loving, considerate, sometimes firm, always good-willed actions are we able to help others in their struggle to become whole and living people.

8. Most of us need a group, led by a person who exemplifies this way of acting, to learn about how we human beings function. It is always wise to remember that groups can be demonic as well as creative. The Hitler youth groups

understood well the principles of group dynamics. We need to pick our group and leader very carefully.

9. In order to implement the suggestion for reading, I propose four books which tell us about what makes us tick. The first of these is Frances Wickes' *The Inner World of Childhood.* It shows clearly and well how children are shaped by the conscious and unconscious attitudes of the adults with whom they live. My students often wondered if they wanted children after they read this book. They were frightened when they realized the influence parents have on children. The second is the slim volume I have already mentioned by Adolf Guggenbuhl-Craig, *Power in the Helping Professions.* The author shows clearly that we seldom have a positive influence upon others unless we treat them as peers and in a loving way. The other two books are by C. G. Jung. In his autobiography, *Memories, Dreams, Reflections,* he demonstrates the theory of personality which we have just described by telling the story of his own inner life. It is one of the truly great books of the twentieth century. In *Modern Man in Search of a Soul* Jung sketches out the fundamentals of a psychology which fits hand and glove with the Christian understanding of human beings.

If we cannot find a professional person with whom to discuss these matters or if we cannot find a group in which to learn, we can always find a faithful friend with whom we can communicate, one who is wise, understanding and has done as much reading as we have. If we would grow, we need this kind of fellowship. We need someone with whom we can discuss our ideas, someone who will be honest with us and tell us when we are off the track in thought or actions.

Loving Through Understanding Psychological Types

One of the most important contributions of C. G. Jung to modern psychological thought is his theory of personality types. That theory has been elaborated on and developed by others. A pen and pencil personality type indicator has been developed by Isabel Briggs-Myers which gives a good picture of the type of person that we probably are. Whatever else we do in trying to understand personality types, we should *not* try to read Jung's monumental study, *Psychological Types.* This book is important but requires a lot of background if it is to be understood.

Jung's basic idea is quite simple. There are different aspects of the total universe in which we live. Some people are more interested in one aspect of it and others in a different aspect. Extroverts are essentially interested in the outer world of things and people. They are energized by frequent interaction, quick action and communication. Introverts, on the other hand, are more interested in the inner world of ideas and concepts. They seem to need time for privacy and time to go into the depth. They also seem to be energized in quiet and during their time alone. We all have the ability to use both of these attitudes, but we usually have a preference for one of them and develop a deeper understanding and use of the one we prefer.

In addition we have four different ways of responding to, relating to and dealing with that world of experience which we choose as our primary concern. Jung believed that these four functions formed two pairs of polar opposites. A diagram will help:

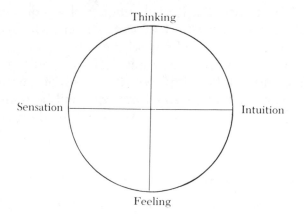

Thinking and feeling are known as the judgmental or decision-making functions, sensation and thinking as the perceptive functions. If our primary way of dealing with the universe is that of thinking, we are interested in arranging the data of our experience according to a logical pattern; if feeling (or valuing) is our most developed function, we are interested in putting such data into a pattern according to our value system or how they relate to human beings. People whose primary function is either thinking or feeling are more interested in arranging data than in collecting it and are often organizers.

If, however, we are more interested in gathering data than in putting it into pattern or order, then we respond to the world either through our sensing ability or through intuition. We get our satisfaction by gathering concrete data until it comes out of our pores or by collecting unconscious data, possibilities, cues, hints, intuitions.

Most of us have developed one of these two attitudes toward the world and one of these four functions. And then we develop another helping or auxiliary function. When all possible combinations are considered, we find that there are sixteen types which can be differentiated from each other. However, these types often blend into one another inasmuch as each of us is a unique combination of these attitudes and functions.

However, we do treat the world in different ways, and unless we have done some careful, critical study, we are likely to assume that all other people respond as we do *and we are likely to expect other people to act in a way that may be alien to them.* If we are to care for or love other people, we certainly will need to help them develop their own type potential and relate to them in a way which is meaningful to them. All types are of value and each of us needs to develop his or her own individual bent. It is very difficult for us to love a spouse, a child, a student or a friend unless we recognize that their type structure may be different from ours. Then we will try to communicate with them in ways which are meaningful to them. Let's take a brief look at the qualities characteristic of each function.

People with a developed sensation function are usually characterized by simplicity in life style. They are interested in concrete facts and seldom in fairy tale or fantasy. They are the getter-doners in the world. Without them the world would cease to go around. When my secretary of twenty years took the indicator and found that she was a sensation type she exclaimed: "Now I see why I was never interested in dolls and put the doll clothes on the dog. At least the dog was real."

The basic interest of the intuitive type is in acquiring wisdom. Such people are the thinker-uppers. Fantasy and fairy tale turn them on. Possibilities stimulate them. However, routine tasks bore them and they often do not follow through. They need new challenges, new problems, variety and change. Sometimes it is difficult for them to make up their minds for there are so many more possibilities.

The thinking type is usually interested in justice. These people want things understandable and in logical order. They do not like exceptions to rules, often act before all the data is in, and make excellent engineers. Often they make good executives because the good of the whole takes precedence over individual desires. They can make decisions, but sometimes their apparent coldness alienates other types.

The feeling type is most often characterized by an ability to experience joy. It is important to realize that the word "feeling" is a translation of a German word, has a meaning different from the usual one, and signifies our capacity to evalute data according to human values. These people are interested in other human beings and what influences them. They are excellent at getting along with others and are often found in the helping professions. Making unpleasant decisions affecting the lives of others is difficult for them.

It is impossible for teachers to teach adequately unless they know their own type structure and realize that other people react to the world differently than they do. Each type is motivated differently. One tragedy of our school system is that reading, writing and arithmetic are intuitive and thinking skills. The other functions are often not valued in our society. Intelligence tests evaluate abilities in only thinking and intuition, and children who are gifted in feeling and in sensation are often given a raw deal in school. Statistics show that sensation types are the first to

140

become discouraged in school and are the first to drop out at every level. *It is impossible to love others unless we can recognize their type and place an adequate value upon their primary function. We should never try to have other persons change their type.* They will do best if they develop what they natively are.

Often different (though seldom opposite) types are drawn together in marriage. It is as if nature were trying to make one complete entity. Children are seldom the same as either parent. My wife and I had been married for twenty years when Ollie Backus introduced us to the Myers-Briggs Personality Type Indicator. We had both been through considerable psychological analysis. However, we learned more about our personal relationship from the results of this one indicator than in most of our previous study. We knew ourselves pretty well, but we did not know the other person. My wife was primarily a feeling-sensation type person, and I was largely an intuitive-thinking type. When we realized how different we were, we realized that the other person was not trying to be difficult; each of us was just different. The other person perceived, experienced and reacted differently to the same situation. When my wife did not understand what bothered me about the innuendos in my stepmother's letters, then I realized that she did not perceive this intuitive data. I also realized that my lack of feeling function had put impossible tensions upon our children who were all feeling types like my wife. I needed to change in order to relate to them.

My wife and I now put on conferences only together. The theory and practice of understanding types is her expertise. We usually offer this indicator to those who come to our conferences. Most people are very interested in learning about themselves. Understanding types also helps in communication skills whether in families, at work, or among those other people at the conference. This knowledge helps people find their true interests and so relieves them of the frustration of doing something alien to their nature. It is a great help in finding a vocation. Our personality type also determines to a large extent the kind of prayer

141

life which is most congenial and creative for us. Most people find the knowledge of types a great help in loving themselves and others.

At one conference before our present team effort I gave a simplified questionnaire to demonstrate how different we were in our type structure. Forty people were present. They represented each type, as the following chart indicates.

	Primary Function	Second	Third	Fourth
Sensation	2	3	15	19
Feeling	22	9	8	1
Thinking	2	10	13	15
Intuition	14	18	14	5

We have learned that it is the feeling and intuitive types who usually attend our conferences. We have also learned that the church is not doing much to reach out to sensation and thinking types. Christian love would seem to suggest that we reach out to all types as a church and as individuals.[1]

What Different Values We Have!

Value clarification teaches us that human beings have very different values as well as being different in the basic ways in which they perceive and relate to the world. Even human beings with much the same background will assess people and their actions in very different ways. When it is my purpose to show a group of people how differently they see the world, I usually tell a modified value clarification story and then ask people to react to the characters in the story. Let me tell the story and give the same instructions that I give to a group at a conference. In this way we can see the variety of responses that are obtained within a group and the readers can compare their responses with others who have shared in this experience of value clarification.

The story begins as most good stories begin. Once upon a time there was a wide and languid river winding its way through a primitive, tropical country. The river was so heavily infested with alligators that no one would survive long in it. The natives were so primitive that they did not know how to use boats. Several generations before, a conquering nation took over this region which was rich in spices and minerals. These advanced people had built a bridge across the river, known as Alligator River. When the invaders departed, one of the few remains of their culture was the bridge which spanned the stream.

On one side of the river, not far from the bridge, a young maiden by the name of Mary lived in a little grass hut. On the other side of the river dwelling in his bamboo cabin was a young man named John. These two young people lived comfortably off the bountiful land and year by year they grew older. When they were quite young they hardly noticed each other, but one spring they suddenly saw each other for the first time. They found themselves walking out onto the bridge for the strangest reasons and standing there talking about all sorts of things. In time Eros shot his poisoned arrows and they fell madly in love. They looked deep into each other's eyes, held hands, and decided to get married. (This story took place in a very different culture than our own.)

And then tragedy struck this peaceful country. A great storm dropped a torrential rainfall that swelled the river to many times its normal size and swept away the bridge, but left all the alligators. Mary and John could no longer meet in the middle of the bridge and exchange the confidences of love. All they could do was stand on the abutments of the former bridge and wave at one another, tears in their eyes. They could think of no way to cross the barrier which divided them.

One day out of the north a strange thing came riding down the river. It was a sailboat. Mary had never seen one before. In the boat was another young man by the name of Steve. He was exploring the lower reaches of Alligator River for his advanced nation which lived many miles up the stream. He saw Mary standing by the riverside gazing across the water and thought to himself: "There is a truly beautiful woman." Turning his boat toward the shore, he stepped out onto the sand a few feet from Mary. When he noticed that she was very sad, he asked her what had happened to make her so unhappy. She told him the story of her love for John and the tragic fate created by the storm and the flood. When she had finished, Steve spoke up. "I am a forthright man. I am aware of my needs and desires. You are very attractive to me. If you will spend the night with me, I will take you across the river and you can be with John. I don't want to force you into a quick decision. I will return in three days and you can give me your answer at that time." Then Steve sailed off.

Mary was very troubled. There was nothing that she wanted more than to cross the waters and be with John, but she belonged to a culture which believed that women should be virgins when they came to marriage. All night long she tossed and turned, and then she remembered that a wise, old woman by the name of Martha lived a few hours' walk from her hut. She decided she would go to talk to Martha.

Martha received her very graciously and asked her what was on her mind. The verbatim report of the conversation went something like this:

Mary: I am deeply troubled.

Martha: I hear you saying that something is bothering you.

Mary: I am confused. I want to cross over to see my beloved, and the only way that I can do it is by violating my principles.

Martha: You feel caught between a sense of love and a sense of duty, and you feel confused.

Mary: I feel confused and upset and don't know what to do.

Martha: You are all torn up inside by this conflict and have lost your perspective.

And so the conversation continued for fifty minutes. Mary returned home realizing how confused she was, but with no idea of what she would do when Steve returned in two days. She finally concluded that what she wanted more than anything else was to be with John, and so she decided that she would take Steve up on his offer. Steve arrived. They spent the night together, and the next morning, true to his agreement, Steve deposited Mary on the river bank not far from John's cabin.

John ran forward with open arms to greet his beloved. Mary was so glad to see John that she immediately spilled out the whole story of what had happened to her and what she had to endure to cross Alligator River. John was incensed, pushed her away and said, "Away from me, you faithless woman! How dare you come to me after defiling yourself with another man! I never want to see you again. Out of my sight!"

And so Mary wandered off weeping on the road on the other side of the river. Within an hour she met David walking along the road. He was about her age, and when he saw that she had been crying and asked her what was troubling her, she told him the whole story. When she finished, David said: "Mary, you stay right here. I am going to take care of John for treating you so badly. Then I will return and we will be married." David left, went down the road, found John, whipped him soundly and then returned. He and Mary were married and lived happily ever after.

Now take a piece of paper and in a column write down the names of the five characters who play a part in this story. Put a (5) behind the name of the person that you like the least and a (1) behind the name of the character whom you like the most. Then rank order the rest of the people in this drama. Place a (4) next to the person whom you find second most unpleasant, a (3) next to the character about whom you feel nearly neutral, and a (2) beside the one whom you like second best. In rank ordering the dramatis personae of this tale, you are really describing your values. Some of the values which the characters embody are listed below:

Mary—naive, human, loving, frailty

John—morality, justice, righteousness, judging

Martha—non-judgmental reflection, listening, unimaginative, stupidity

Steve—honest, frank instinctuality, selfishness, oppor-
tunistic

David—aggressiveness, retribution, protection, violence

Most of the people gathered at the Christmas retreat
at Pecos, New Mexico, came from a similar background.
They were all very decent persons. All were seeking to
grow in the Christian life, and yet look how differently they
valued the people of this story.

Below we give the rank orderings which occurred at
that retreat. This is exactly as Joan Liebler took it down for
me. The figures do not add up because some of the people
probably found it uncomfortable to raise their hands when
they discovered the majority viewed one character far differently than they did. We have discovered that we obtain
a truer picture if we ask people to close their eyes when
they tell what rank they have given to each of these people.

	Highest				Lowest
	1	2	3	4	5
John	3	8	13	30	42
Mary	31	47	17	6	2
Steve	9	4	25	31	25
Martha	8	10	42	25	20
David	52	25	9	5	7

We cannot love other people until we can accept them
and their values as they are. This is not easy when I view
Mary as the best of the characters and someone I am talking to views her as the worst. We are often sensitive about
our values. My wife and I have different values. Our values
are expressed in what we do, and this can cause conflict.
Only as we have come to know what our values are, and
how different they are, and to talk about them, have we
been able to deal with these conflicts creatively. Knowing
about our own values and respecting the values of others is
a first step in loving those close to us as well as others.
There is no one Christian value system.

Usually people will not even begin to reveal themselves until they are assured that we can listen to and accept their values without judging. Feeling types in particular need counselors who basically have the same values. Accepting different sets of values is a first step toward communication and love.

9

Loving the Acquaintance

Most social and religious groups tell us that we should have a special concern for all those within the group of which we are a part. The Old Testament states this explicitly. In the Book of the Law, Leviticus, the Israelites were told to love all other Israelites in these words: "You shall love your neighbor as yourself" (Leviticus 19:18) The great Hebrew prophets thundered against their people when they did not take this precept seriously.

Jesus, however, takes this statement from the Torah and gives it a greatly expanded application. In the Gospel of Luke we are told that an expert in the law was trying to trap Jesus by asking him what course of action was necessary to obtain eternal life. In good Socratic fashion Jesus asked the scribe what he thought. He replied with the classic Hebrew summary of the law: "You must love God with all your heart, with all your soul, with all your strength, and with all your mind; you must love your neighbor as yourself." After Jesus agreed, the scribe, in order to justify himself, asked: "And who is my neighbor?" Jesus then told the story of the rescue by a Samaritan of a Jew who had fallen among thieves. One important point of this story is that all human beings are our neighbors, even our most despised enemies.

The requirement to care for all people, universal love, is a new idea on the religious scene and a difficult one to accept and follow. The question quite naturally arises: How can I love everyone? In the next four chapters we will deal with some of the specifics which are involved when we try to love the acquaintance, the enemy, the stranger and the oppressed.

First of all it is perfectly clear that if we take on every cause and every person we would drive ourselves to distraction or wear ourselves out without accomplishing very much. We need to look at ourselves and see what our special gifts are, what needs we can reach out to and what bundles God seems to place in our baskets. Agnes Sanford always tries to remember to ask God whether an engagement has her name on it before she accepts it and whether she is guided to pray for healing when she has a request for help. When we try to love everyone in the abstract, we often end up by loving no one concretely and in particular. We need some guidance in order to discern what we are going to undertake, what is our responsibility. A time of quiet prayer and journal reflection is often necessary if we are going to set sensible priorities and limits.

Loving Employees—A Practical Example

It was not a religious professional who opened my eyes to what it meant to love all those with whom my life brought me in contact. It was a businessman, Jack Smith, the president of a medium-sized manufacturing plant. The business had been started by his father and had grown. Finally the tension of running the business became too much for the father, and so it was turned over to his son. Things continued to go well after World War II, but then for several reasons the market began to shrink and the quality of the product began to deteriorate.

One day in the midst of these difficulties Jack Smith was in the factory trying to adjudicate between two employees who were arguing about whether it was too hot or too cold. This was the final straw. He left the factory, went into his office, closed the door, sat down at his desk, and

149

said to himself, "I can't run this business. I don't know what to do. I guess I can either get drunk or I can pray." He thought a little while longer and then reflected quietly: "Probably nothing will change if I pray. If I get drunk, I'll have a hangover and nothing will change. However, if I pray and nothing comes of it, I can always get drunk later on." With this deep conviction he put his head down on his hands and said, "Okay, Lord, I can't run this business any longer. What should I do?"

He was quiet a few moments and suddenly these words shot through his head in rapid fire: "Create the conditions whereby individuals can develop to the maximum of their capacities within the opportunities at hand." He was thunderstruck and responded out loud: "What was that, Lord?" This time the same sentence spoke itself in slowly measured words in his mind. He wrote it down. I have never come across a better description than this of the way to treat employees, employers, students, teachers, members of the Holy Name Society, or people in the PTA. Our task is to provide an atmosphere, as much as it is within our hands to do so, in which other people can grow, become, rise to their potential.

Jack Smith was impressed by this experience. He did not realize at that time that the insight which had come to him was also the most recent management theory developed by professional managers in business. He decided, however, that if God could still speak, he should take the New Testament seriously. He started almost immediately to examine it carefully, and he read it through seven times. After doing so, he began to realize that this answer to his prayer made sense. The company was little more than the people who worked there, and if each of them was working, thinking, creating at top potential, then the company would grow and prosper. His task as primary influence in this organization was to create an atmosphere in which human beings could grow and develop. He also realized that this principle applied not only to the employees whom he liked, or who liked him, but to all of those who worked at the company.

Eleven Suggestions for Love in Action

But how was he to create that climate of attitude among his employees? For many months he allowed his new insight to ferment in the depth of him. Gradually he came to the conclusion that he must apply as many of Christ's teachings to the practical everyday concerns of his business as possible. This would not only be good business; it would also be Christianity in action, love actualized in that situation. One day as he was reflecting, eleven rules emerged into his consciousness. Here is his list:

1. Serve those whom you expect to serve you.

2. Consider no person inferior, but recognize limitations.

3. Lead men and women by action and example.

4. Be humble in speaking about your accomplishments.

5. Teach and be taught.

6. Attack unfairness from any quarter.

7. Believe that your employees must prosper if you are to prosper.

8. Seek the truth no matter who may get hurt.

9. Pray for God's guidance when you must make a decision affecting the life and future of any person.

10. Make your own decision based on your own best judgment only after careful consideration has been given to *all* the facts.

11. Forgive honest mistakes where the person making the mistake is honestly self-critical. If people are not self-critical, they must learn to be or they can never successfully supervise others or develop to their best abilities.

This is quite a set of suggestions. In effect they provide a base for treating human beings as persons rather than as objects, as *thou* rather than *it*. These ideas have been successfully tested by this company as a basis for both personal and industrial growth. Let's look at some of the implications of these rules.

First, by seeing ourselves as serving, we will develop along with others in the group. We also need to look honestly at individuals and their personal abilities—not just judging them according to the positions they fill or by comparing their results with what *we* do. It is our job to examine our own actions, our own example, and to try to understand the actions of others in the context of the total situation in which we work. We can neither toot our own horn nor force others into impossible roles beyond their limitations. We need to teach by our own example, and listen, watch and learn from each individual. To do this, individuals must be treated as persons who can grow and develop in their own right. Most of us do not start to develop freely until we are treated in this way by someone who wants to share experience and knowledge.

On the other hand, it hurts the individual, as well as souring group relations, for us to tolerate unfairness from any source. And if we are truly fair, we will want others to prosper as we are trying to. Equally, to put our own or anyone else's judgment about persons or things above the truth causes unfairness, and the individuals are hurt far worse than if the facts are sought and truth is faced squarely. Who do we think we are to make our own truth? When we do this, we make ourselves more than God and reality. Indeed, how much injury and pain and misunderstanding would be avoided if we insisted on these two standards of fairness and truth. And the only place to start is with our own determination to seek the facts and to pray to God from the depth of our being whenever we must come to a decision affecting human beings. If we will seek the truth and listen to what comes in the silent recesses of the soul as we wait in quiet, we will usually come to understand what is the best course of action for all concerned.

Finally, when we give others the freedom to make mistakes, we give them the freedom to grow. It is often only by our mistakes—which all of us make—that we grow and develop. We need to offer forgiveness and also to help others to understand and evaluate their own actions. By developing a self-critical understanding of themselves people begin to grow to the fullness of their abilities. Without forgiveness, men and women stop growing because they are afraid to make mistakes. Without critical evaluation they do not profit from their mistakes.

These principles actually did create an atmosphere in which individuals grew and developed as the company grew and prospered. This is not just a business success story. The important moral to this story is that seriously opening ourselves to the voice of God and trying to put caring principles to work can change the spiritual climate and moral atmosphere of any group of which we are a part. This is particularly true of any group in which we are the primary influence.

Most neighborhoods would be delightful places to live in if these simple, basic suggestions were followed. Most churches would be truly redeeming fellowships if clergy and congregation agreed to put these rules into action. The last five years while I was pastor of a large congregation we tried to use these suggestions in the parish. They worked. I have found that using these principles as a base for the classroom created an open atmosphere where most students were eager to learn.

Of course these suggestions need to be varied and applied to the specific situations in which we find ourselves. However, I know of no better way to try to love the acquaintance, the person with whom I am casually and not intimately related, than to create the conditions whereby

153

individuals may develop to the maximum of their potential within the opportunities at hand. I know of no better guidelines for implementing this goal than those which my friend, Jack Smith, shared with me nearly twenty years ago. This story also reminds us that it is dangerous to ask God for advice, for he may well answer.

10

Loving the Enemy

Jesus believed that real ascent on the spiritual way does not begin until we start to love our enemies, those who mistreat us, those who spitefully use us. There is no question that Jesus said it and taught it and lived it. *We are not to love the enemy instead of the friend and family and acquaintance, but in addition to them.* Other loving is a preparation for this supreme effort. And let no one think that it is not difficult to sincerely love the enemy.

It almost seems unnatural to say that we can love those who persecute us. How can we love those whom we do not like? Is it not hypocrisy, pure and unadulterated, to profess that we love those whom we do not even enjoy being near? It is not hypocrisy; it is the way of tension and growth. Starr Daily, who certainly knew what it was to have lots of enemies after years in and out of prison, used to tell me that it was not his friends who made him grow, but his enemies. He had to grow to encompass them.

One conventional way of avoiding the strong medicine of the gospel of love is to maintain that I can love people that I don't like. I don't have to like everyone, but I must love them. Let me say very clearly and simply that loving without liking is not loving at all. Please deliver me from the love of people who do not like me. Genuine love is a quality of caring which finds something appealing in the other person as well as making the heroic effort to "love." We are beginning to follow the way of love, the way of Christ, when our loving and our liking begin to converge. This does not imply that we approve of everything that other people are doing, for they may be causing harm and hurt. But we can still care for them and love them.

How can I begin to love and like my enemy? What can I do to enable me to start toward this seemingly impossible goal? Years of struggling with my own dislikes and fears and angers and hates have produced six suggestions which usually help when I put my energy into working at them.

Facing Our Anger and Hurts

The first absolutely necessary step in starting to love the enemy is to recognize that at present we do not register very high on the loving-the-enemy scale. Not only are there people we don't like very well, people we avoid, people we strike back at; we don't even show an unrelenting effort to love those who are close to us. Often the enemy will pop up right in our own family. There is a lovely quip that one reason children and grandparents get along so well is that they have a common enemy. It is rather shocking to observe how little love we have in our hearts and our lives, how little of our action and behavior is determined by our desire to "like-love" those around us.

One of the most virulent forms of rejection is avoiding people. Usually studiously avoiding other persons or ignoring them is more hostile and violent than blowing up at them or striking them with our hand. We human beings are social creatures; many of us wither and die when we are out of contact with other humans. In many cultures, banishment from the country or the social group was considered nearly on par with a death sentence.

Some years ago my son and some of his friends decided that they would play a trick on one of the members of their little group at school. They carefully, assiduously avoided speaking to this young man from the time they arrived in

156

the morning, and as the day went on, the young man became more and more disturbed. When he left at three o'clock before school was out, he was physically ill. My son and his friends were very much ashamed of themselves and they apologized later, but they learned how important they were to one another. There is probably no way we can hurt others more than by subtly turning our backs upon them.

There can be no growth in Christian love until we reflect how little caring there is in most of us much of the time. Then we need to decide to try to do better. This is the only way that the finer flowers of love can ever begin to bloom in our lives. We can make a beginning by recognizing that our acts of love are rather puny and having the determination to be more heroic in the way of love.

There is one group of people who are very hard for me to love. These are the people who come up to me at a conference when I am talking about love and smile with saccharine sweetness, saying, "But I don't know what you are talking about. I love everyone and everyone loves me." Except for those cases of first-class saints (and I have met but few in my travels up and down the highways of the world), these people are examples of pure unconsciousness. They are simply unaware of their own inner murderers and inner idiots.

Sometimes our very attempt to love and advance on the spiritual way will actually gain enmity from others. A friend reminded me that Jesus was hung on a cross, most of the prophets were persecuted, Socrates was fed hemlock, and most of the saints came close to condemnation before they were accepted as true saints. There is a touching and realistic scene in one of Charles Williams' poems. When Parsifal meets Lancelot, his somewhat erring father, he asks Lancelot's forgiveness for having lived such an exemplary life, for he knows that it must have added to his father's guilt and pain.

Love sometimes involves suffering just as it did for Jesus. Dr. Joseph Needham expressed this truth incomparably in a sermon which he preached before the University of Oxford. He spoke not only as a Christian layman but also as one of the world's greatest biochemists. Here are his reflections:

> I have spoken already about cosmic love and love among us at the human level, but love is vulnerable, inevitably doomed to suffering, if it were only on account of the terrible fact of transience itself. There is rejection, there is unkindness, there is cruelty, there is evanescence, there is coldness. Anything may happen. In our religion we believe that Christ dared to let go and emptied himself of divine glory when he, the Tao, became incarnate in a human body. Love was denied, love was betrayed, love was crucified—and love was undefeated. That was the "Way" of the cross. That was the Truth about human relationships, and that was the Life which all men and women must lead if the patterns of the Tao are to be fulfilled on earth. And so we come back to our starting-point and look again at the Way or Tao of love expressed in that wonderful collect: "O God, who has taught us that all our doings without love are nothing worth, send down thy Holy Spirit and pour into our hearts that most excellent gift of love, the very bond of peace and of all virtues, without which whosoever liveth is counted dead before thee."[1]

It is important to realize that enemies are those who do not like us, as well as those whom we do not like. Jesus told us to leave our gift at the altar if we remembered that someone had something against us. We should go and be reconciled and then present our gift.

Often within the Christian family as well as in Christian groups—in guilds and sodalities, in parish councils and vestries, in coffee hours and church suppers—there is an unashamed lack of Christian love. This tragic lack turns many people away from Christianity. Indeed people sometimes even pride themselves on the fact that they have deep and well-rooted animosities within them. It is one thing for us to have them (all of us do); it is quite another to be proud of them. The first step then in our attempt at loving the enemy is to realize that we have enemies. This helps us see where we are in our journey toward Christian wholeness and where we really want to be.

Stopping Our Actions of Anger and Vengeance

The second step toward loving the enemy is equally simple. Without it there can be no increase in our spiritual temperature. That step consists of ceasing to do anything unkind to the enemy. This is so obvious that it should not even be necessary to suggest it. As long as we express our anger or hostility in punitive action, in reprisal or in any form of attack, financial, physical or psychological, there is no hope that our "love-liking" toward that person will increase. These actions wear deeper the rut of our anger so that the wheels of our lives are less able to get out of the groove of hostility. Acts of retribution feed the fire of hatred.

And yet anger is a perfectly natural reaction to the injury and wrong which we so often suffer. Someone kicks me in the shins and I immediately mobilize my entire being so I can kick him or her back, and a little harder to boot. If a neighbor sweeps leaves into our yard, our natural tendency is to go and sweep them right back, and a few more along with them. If my wife complains about something I have done, I look for some worse failing in her and complain back. If people hurt our feelings, we either try to return the hurt or else we turn our backs and quite pointedly give them the cold shoulder.

Jesus told us that we should turn the other cheek and go the second mile with one who forced us to go one mile. He was trying to dramatize the fact that if we are to grow in love, we simply have to cease our destructive actions before we can focus in the right direction. When we begin to consider the possibility of living by these statements from Jesus, at least we will stop our actions of retribution.

Most of us are quite civilized in public. We seldom go at each other with bric-a-brac, fists or knives. Of course the law strongly discourages this in most countries. It is shocking, however, that this kind of violence still takes place within the confines of supposed domestic tranquility. What we wouldn't think of doing at the club we do at home. Police find that intervening in domestic quarrels is their most dangerous duty other than tracking down violent criminals. Most of our public cruelty to one another is not outwardly violent, but rather legal, subtle and very refined. Such aggression is as destructive as a physical attack. Our second step in developing in love for the enemy is to realize that we are indulging in violent actions of one kind or another *and bring them to a halt.*

Even as we realize that we need to bring our unloving actions to a halt, we also need to recognize that anger is a necessary part of being human and can be a source of energy. Anger has dozens of different names. When we are hurt or threatened, we usually have the impulse toward either flight or fight. Anger is the mobilization of our entire being to attack what is threatening us. We often pay a deadly price when we try to forget, repress or ignore our anger.

Emotions are those human responses in which a physical and bodily reaction goes along with a set of feelings. When we are angry our bodies prepare for action; the bronchial tubes open up to let in more oxygen, the blood sugar is released to provide fuel for the oxygen to burn, and both heart beat and blood pressure increase to race this energy through the body. The blood clotting time goes down to prepare for a possible injury. When my friend Tommy Tyson, the well-known evangelist, listened to a recital of the physical affects of anger, he reacted spontaneously with these words: "I can't afford to sit on my anger and let it seethe. It will destroy me. Doing that is immoral."

When bottled up, unfaced anger, resentment, and hostility can cause social chaos. The blood feud which is endemic in some societies is a perfect example of this. Any little event can trigger a monumental reaction. Continued hatred can cause psychological tension leading to bitterness, isolation and disaster. And, lastly, repressed hostility can erode our physical bodies as a heavy rain erodes a bare hillside.

And what can I do to keep this inner energy released in a creative and positive manner? First of all I need to see that anger, except in certain cases of physical danger, seldom produces positive results. I remember a woman many years ago who pointed to her bony middle finger and exclaimed proudly: "That is a sign that I never forgive or let go of a resentment." As long as I hang onto my anger consciously I am not putting all of me into the following of Christ and I am putting myself in a dangerous position religiously, socially, psychologically, and physically.

As I have outlined in dealing with hostility within the family, there are things I can do to get my anger under control. I can write down my anger, concretize it, put it out before me and see what it looks like in black and white as if it were someone else's bitterness. I can talk it over with a friend. I can look for an outer cause of the anger and change what is upsetting me. Sometimes I find that there is little or nothing I can do about a situation which causes anger and resentment down to the marrow of my soul. Then, like Job, I can cry out to God from the depth of my agony. At such times I usually feel the presence of God very keenly and know that I have come into contact with one who is able to bear the burden of my anger and distress. As the crucified one, God knew this agony himself. When I have protested specifically to God about the abyss which so often reaches up to suck me down into it, I have found that the pain and anger have often subsided by the next day and the abyss has less power to touch me.

There is no sin in being angry. The sin is to pretend it is not there or to let it out whenever we feel it or to nurse anger in our relationships, feeding it more and more grievances without facing the acutal situation honestly and squarely. Nursed anger becomes hate. Then love is entirely defeated in us because hate is the zero of love. Paul wrote to the Ephesians, "Even if you are angry, you must not sin; never let the sun set on your anger or else you will give the devil a foothold" (Ephesians 4:26). If we are to defeat the anger of the murderer within we will need to renounce the murderer's way and bring our best effort to bear on changing our pattern of action, replacing the natural angry reac-

161

tion with a more positive one. The outer enemy often reveals to me my inner murderer and his or her power better than another person.

One of the reasons that the Christian church conquered the ancient world was that it actually practiced this kind of attitude toward the enemy. The martyrs went to the arena without cursing and breathing vengeance upon the spectators. The seed of the church was the blood of the martyrs. Often the spectators at the arena were stupefied. The Christians thrown to the beasts actually handled their torments as Jesus did on the cross. St. Perpetua was martyred by wild beasts in North Africa in the first part of the second century. When she was asked why she did not curse the informers, the judge, those who were about to put her into the arena and those gathered to watch, she replied, "They already suffer from the attack of the evil one. I would not want to add to their burden with my curses."

Bridling the Tongue

The next suggestion for loving the enemy is an extension of the last one. It concerns a problem so common and so often considered harmless that it requires special attention. Whenever I gossip negatively about others, I am treating them as the enemy. One of the ten commandments tells us that we should not bear false witness against our neighbor. This could well be translated: We shall not gossip.

Not only does my unkind action wear deeper the rut of my ugliness, but *my unkind talking about other people does exactly the same thing.* I personally find this step very difficult. The tongue at times seems to have a life all of its own. And yet how I dislike it when I find that others have been discussing me in a critical or gossipy way. When there is a group moral dissection of someone going on and I have a juicy morsel which I could add, I cannot tell it without damaging myself. That kind of gossip pushes me away from my goal of love.

I know of only two valid reasons for saying an unkind or critical remark about another person. In the first case my inner feelings of critical anger are hurting me so much that I need to discharge them. However, such things should be expressed to a priest or a spiritual friend and not vented in the heat of the moment. The other reason is that we truly believe that the actions of these people may be hurting other persons or themselves and that they need help. In Matthew 17 we are given detailed instructions on how to handle the latter situation. First of all we are to go to such people directly and see if we can come to an understanding with them. If this does not work, then we are to take two or three with us and try the same method. This failing, we are to go to the church in order to clear up the circumstances which are causing the problem. And last of all, if the others will not listen to us, we are to treat them as tax gatherers. We should remember at this point, however, how Jesus treated *them!* He treated them with love and charity and went out to them. They even became his disciples.

This is excellent advice. Early in my ministry a note which I had written to a woman from the parish was mistaken for a telegram. A religious leader added two and two, got twenty-two, and concluded that something was going on between me and this woman at the seminary. Instead of coming directly to me, he went to the bishop, who went to the dean, who talked to my wife, who had helped write the note and knew all about it. Had the dean and the bishop not had confidence in me, the situation could have been very unpleasant. The suggestions of Jesus in Matthew 5 could have nipped this problem in the bud. They are very practical, but it takes courage to implement them.

I have not always seen the importance of bridling the tongue. Indeed, I regret to say, when I was in seminary one of my favorite indoor pastimes was picking apart other seminarians, professors and high-placed clerics. This kind of action seemed to prevail as a general entertainment. No one suggested that it wasn't exactly the Christian way. As I went into my first parish the practice continued. It seemed to give me a sense of wisdom and superiority to be able to uncover and dissect the moral tumors of other, particularly successful clergy in the diocese.

I well remember my moment of enlightenment in this

matter. I had performed a wedding and was in the process of taking some of the flowers out to the reception at the bride's home. Helping me was a member of the altar guild who told me that she had been reading *Unity*, a publication I had never viewed with high theological regard. Somehow the conversation turned to gossip and my friend said: "I have learned from *Unity* that I have no right to speak negatively or judgingly about any other human being." I was shaken, for I knew instantly that she was right and that *Unity* was right in this matter. Gossip usually proceeds out of sheer maliciousness, arrogance, cowardice, lack of self-esteem, and pride. It may well be a worse breach of the law than the sins of the flesh like adultery, which sometimes has a grain of love within it.

From that day on I have tried to keep my negative criticism to myself. I have often failed, but then I try to get up again without flailing myself with remorse, and try again. As pastor in one congregation for twenty years, I came to realize that there can be no real growth in love toward any specific person, or growth in love in general, until we cease talking about other people. Doing unkindnesses and saying them create a climate in which love does not grow.

St. Teresa of Avila speaks of the vital importance of this rule for all on the religious way:

> But the safe path for the soul that practices prayer will be not to bother about anything or anyone and to pay attention to itself and pleasing God. This is important—ah, if I should have to speak of the mistakes I have seen happen by trusting in good intentions! But let us strive always to look at virtues and good deeds we see in others and cover their defects with the thought of our own great sins. This is a manner of acting that, although we cannot do so with perfection right away, gradually gains for us a great virtue, that is: considering all others better than ourselves.[2]

164

Praying for the Enemy

In the fourth step we move from the things we cease doing to the things we need to do to encourage love. I find that praying for the people whom I dislike and the ones who dislike me has both a practical and metaphysical effect. In my journal I keep a list of people for whom I pray. I have listed there those who are particularly important to me, those who are sick, those who have asked for prayer, *and those who might be called enemies.* I scatter these people with whom I have trouble all throughout the list. In this way if my prayer list falls into others' hands, they will be no wiser.

The best method of praying in a general way for other people is to pray the Lord's Prayer for them. If John is the one I am praying for, I say: "John's Father who art in heaven, Hallowed be thy name in John, Thy kingdom come in John, Thy will be done in John, on earth just as if he were with you in heaven. Give him his daily bread, all that he needs to sustain and enrich his life. Forgive John and help him to forgive others. Do not put John to the test as he is weak like the rest of us, and please deliver John from the Evil One. Let John's joy be in your kingdom and power and glory forever and ever." While I am praying in this way I visualize John and imagine the Risen Christ with him.

Praying like this for the enemy has several practical effects. If I am asking God to take care of several people and to pour his blessings upon them, this impedes me from saying or doing anything unkind to them. Such negative action would be at odds with what I am asking God to do and would make me a sheer hypocrite. It would put me in the position of saying, "Lord, you take care of John, while I'll fix him here below."

There is also a real power in intercession. For some people it can be their primary vocation. We human beings are in much closer contact with one another than we have been taught to believe by our materialistic world view. The study of parapsychology shows that we have non-sensory ways of reaching out to other people. The Dean of the Engineering School at Princeton sponsored a study of telepathy and energy with one of his students and published the material in the *Princeton Alumni Weekly*. When we deny that our psyches are strangely interrelated, we are closing our minds to observable facts which have been replicated in laboratories all over the world. When we are praying for someone earnestly, imaginatively, something often gets through; space and time do not seem to make much difference. Unfortunately hatred and malice when meditated upon can also get through. This is the basis of truth in witchcraft.[3] Real prayer opens one to a new dimension of reality and can be a channel for the healing love of God.

When I first considered the possible effectiveness of intercession, I decided to take on a difficult project. I picked a woman in the parish who was nasty, cantankerous, gossipy and domineering. Most of the people in the church were afraid of her and her family was terrorized by her. If prayer could help Ethel, I was sure it could help anyone. I began praying for her daily, often using the method which I suggest above. About three weeks later I received a call from Ethel. She wanted to come and see me. In fear and trembling I made the appointment, wondering what kind of trouble was brewing. When she came into my office she flopped down in a chair opposite me and began to cry. She said that she realized what a horrible person she was, but that she just wanted us at the church to know how much the church meant to her and how much worse she would have been without the influence of the clergy and the church upon her life. I realized that she suffered as much being herself as I did being me. From that time we became good friends, and I realized again the truth that in the depth of us we all carry heavy burdens.

Positive Action

If my attempt to love the enemy ceases with prayer, that love will probably not come to fruition. We need prayer *and* action. The fifth suggestion consists of examining the life of the one whom we do not love (or like) and looking long and hard enough to find something positive

166

and creative in that person, something we can genuinely admire. I have discovered that we can find this in everyone. With some people I'll admit it takes much longer, but there are redeeming qualities in everyone.

And then when the opportunity comes, we can simply make the positive observation we have discovered. The effects of such an action can be quite surprising. I remember being in a group of one of the guilds at the church, and the tongues were sharpened for moral dissection. The former president of the guild was on the table for an exploratory moral operation. The list of this person's failings grew and grew until someone remarked, "But did you ever notice what a fine job she has done in raising her son?" It was like a bombshell. The whole tone of the group changed, and the conversation about the woman ceased.

Attorneys tell me that it is difficult for them to defend clients without coming to have a higher regard for them. It is nearly impossible to become another's defender and protector without having our appreciation for him or her increase. When we know a lot about another we realize that all of us are having a hard struggle. This generates at least pity, and pity is close to compassion, and this is not far from love. A ninth-century Islamic mystic, Sai-al-Sakadi, put it so well: "Perfect love exists between two people only when each addresses the other with the words, 'O, myself!' "

The sixth and last suggestion is like the fifth. Let us try to perform some kind act for the persons whom we are trying to love, something that will make them happy. We can watch the individuals, see what would give them joy, and then perform the action, give the gift, provide the situation for those people without their even knowing that we have done it. The effect is often miraculous. It is very difficult, if not impossible, to dislike persons whom we have made happy. It is almost inhuman not to rejoice with others when we have brought them joy. Our gift may be either some small act of consideration or something which requires greater effort, but it makes no difference as long as our action brings happiness to the person. Whenever joy is expressed by others, of course, they become more lovable, too.

In the final analysis it is not the people who do things for us that we love the most, but the people for whom we do things. This is a fundamental psychological law. When others do something for us it often causes us to feel obligated. When we do something for others without any expectations, we are closely in tune with the central core of reality and are sustained and strengthened by Love.

One of the reasons that we love our children so much exemplifies this truth. We have done so much for them, partly because we had to so that they could survive, and also because we wanted to, and also because they needed what we had to give. We share our lives with our children, and in sharing them we participate in Love itself. This kind of giving of ourselves works outside the family group as well as within it. If we try it we may well find that our specific dislikes can turn into love.

As our love begins to grow and increase toward those who have been our enemies, we begin to realize more and more fully the importance and power of love and our need for it.

Someone asked me once what happens when we have dealt with all the enemies in our lives. I replied that we need not worry. God loves us so much and is so interested in our growth that in his infinite mercy and love he will always provide us with a few more!

11

Loving the Stranger

Loneliness destroys human beings, and nothing contributes more to loneliness than being a stranger, being alienated, separated, isolated. Solitary confinement is considered the worst punishment that can be meted out to someone in prison.

Being isolated and alienated is one of the contributing factors in depression. Simple depression has become the common cold of modern psychiatry, afflicting more and more people of every age group, particularly the young. Depression contributes to suicide, which is increasing in most places in the Western world. The second stated cause of death of young men from eighteen to twenty-five is suicide. The first cause of death is accidents, and these are often simply masked suicide.

In addition to all this, James Lynch shows in *The Broken Heart* that single people are much more likely to be strangers than married people and that single people have a much higher mortality rate than those who are married. This applies to nearly every kind of illness. Lynch takes the church to task for not realizing the need that men and women have for fellowship and not placing a top priority on reaching out to the strangers in the community.

Jesus also placed an incredible emphasis on loving the

stranger and reaching out to the forgotten. In Matthew 25 we find these words: "Come and receive the kingdom which has been prepared for you ever since the creation of the world. I was hungry and you fed me, thirsty and you gave me drink; I was a stranger and you received me, naked and you clothed me; I was sick and you took care of me, in prison and you visited me. . . . Whenever you did this for one of the least important of these brothers of mine, you did it for me." And one of the worst things about being hungry, naked and in prison is that we feel that we have been forgotten, that no one cares, that we are strangers.

In our atomized society few people live long in the same community. The sense of social solidarity breaks down as more and more we become strangers to one another. There is no place where this problem is more clear than on our large college campuses. One college leader told me that at no time in history have greater numbers of unrelated human beings been brought together in one spot than on the modern large state university campus. And in no place is there greater loneliness.

Several years ago a suicide occurred on the Notre Dame campus. This is unusual for a Catholic college whose students have been taught that suicide is not an acceptable way of exiting from this world. It is even more unusual at Notre Dame where there is excellent supervision of dormitories with priests, nuns, religious brothers or trained laypeople in residence in each of them. The director of student affairs was troubled and decided to get at the cause of this tragedy. He called in all the students who had attended small classes with the unfortunate student and also interviewed those who lived up and down the hall in the dormitory where the student had lived. He wanted to know what kind of person this student was. What he discovered was that *no one even knew him.* It is little wonder that the young man took his life.

Simply being around other people does not mean that we are escaping loneliness. The worst and most poignant loneliness is found in the rooming house districts of great cities where there are swarms of people, but no relationship or meeting of person with person. On top of this there is often nothing to do, and this usually leads to boredom.

Another place where one finds great loneliness is among the very wealthy. Many of them have found that most of the people who seek them out want only what they have. They feel used rather than related to. It is not physical pain that brings the greatest misery, but psychic pain. Loneliness, alienation, and the sense of being a stranger to others are often a part of psychic pain.

Some people are lonely even in the midst of families. They have not been made to feel that they have value just as they are. They feel rejected and believe that no one truly cares for them. All human relationship seems a mockery. In the best of psychological and religious counseling, one of the goals is to break down the barriers of loneliness. Then we may meet and bring relationship to another person, offering and receiving fresh air for this staleness of the soul.

Many people become disturbed at holiday seasons, especially Thanksgiving and Christmas. They look back into their childhood at this one time when mercy and love seemed to flow generously. As Christmas approaches they look forward with anticipation, hoping that they may capture the same spirit once again. When the miracle does not happen, then their hopes and expectations crash in upon them and they realize what alienated strangers they are. They crumble into the Christmas neurosis, into the unbearable reality of their loneliness.

Seeing Strangers

One does not have to be a professional psychologist in order to reach out to the stranger. All of us can do something. First of all reaching out to the stranger has to have a high priority on our list of activities. We need to realize how life-giving this kind of action can be.

One of the finest tributes I heard about my mother after her death came from a peddler. When he stopped by and found that she had died, he told me that my mother had always welcomed him, had him sit down on the porch, and then brought him a cool drink. They would talk for a while, and perhaps she would buy a few trifles. The man told me that this refreshed him and gave him a sense of being part of the human race once again.

For twenty years I was rector of a large parish in California. One of the most serious problems was the constant influx of new people. It was like ministering to a parade. We talked about integrating these newcomers and welcoming them, but how difficult it was for the parishioners to reach out. They were afraid that they might try to greet some oldtimer who had been around for a long time, only to be told that the oldtimer's grandfather had built the church. Often it is difficult to reach out to others because we do not think they would want anything to do with us if they knew us.

For several years I conducted classes at Notre Dame in a course entitled, "Personal Perspectives in Nonviolence." The director of the Nonviolence Program came to realize that many of the students came into the program for violent reasons and that before they could legitimately work in situations of outer violence they had to deal with their own inner violence. We met in small groups of no more than fifteen. Sometimes I would come into the classroom and say not a word. Often the silence would continue for a half hour or longer before the students could overcome their fear of one another and begin a discussion. So many of us wonder if anyone else really wants anything to do with us. Often our violence springs out of this fear. Someone has remarked that human beings have this in common with dogs—that strangeness intimidates and enrages them.

In her book *Search for Silence*, Elizabeth O'Connor illustrates how often most of us feel like strangers:

In the *New York Times Book Review*, Edward Dahlberg wrote poignantly of lost opportunities for relationship when he reflected on his encounters with Theodore Dreiser. He had longed to know Dreiser, but when he thought of getting in touch with the man, he pictured him engaged in the creation of another Titan. How could he interrupt him? Besides, he imaged himself as a "raw prentice" with nothing of value to offer the great man. "Should I telephone him, he would surely hang up the receiver, and I would be mortally wounded." Finally Dahlberg took the "penultimate hazard." Dreiser asked him to come right to his apartment. Then follow Dahlberg's piercing lines in the story of a relationship that he is uncertain he can call a friendship.

"My meetings with Dreiser continued, but I always was of the mind that I was ravaging his precious hours. Long after his death I read that, at the time we became acquainted, his closest friend had died and he hoped that Edward Dahlberg might take the lost friend's place. What a glut of mulligrubs I had when I perused that single line in a biographical study of Dreiser. Time and again since then I have been bitten by the ever-hungry tooth of remorse. Good God, Theodore Dreiser needed me; and I, who have always been the beggar in any relationship, did not realize how desperately I required him!"[1]

The first step in mobilizing ourselves toward the stranger is realizing the human and religious value of this action. The second is to realize how much of the stranger each of us often feels himself or herself to be. The third step is to look out and see the stranger. This may appear quite simple to do, but it is not as simple as it may sound. In order to see the stranger, we must be aware enough to look beyond ourselves.

We must be conscious enough so that we are not always thinking of ourselves and our circle, our clique, our reactions, our desires. It is difficult for us to be truly aware of the world around us and particularly of the people around us. We usually live with habitual perceptions and according to established patterns. Frequently when we are in a group we gravitate immediately to our own friends and start talking about the latest thing of common interest in our circle.

How seldom do we pause in a group and look around and say to ourselves: "I wonder if there is someone here who is new or lonely, a person who needs my fellowship." Having been strangers in a strange land as the Hebrews were in Egypt can open us up to the pain of being a stranger. Often I have felt uncomfortable in a new group, separated and different. Once, however, I was outwardly a stranger as well. I was in Switzerland and my passport was taken from me because the Swiss government wanted to be sure I did not earn any money in their country without paying taxes. I was an *alien.* I was not a citizen. I did not know my rights. I was a stranger. When the plane landed in Los Angeles I wanted to get down and kiss the ground. I was home. I was no longer a stranger. The worst thing about prison is that we have lost our rights; we have become strangers. The forgotten, the sick, the hungry feel the same way.

We do not like to be aware of the fact that we are often strangers in the midst of strangers. Have you ever noticed what happens when a group of strangers get onto an elevator? We treat each other like *strangers.* We don't look at each other. We might think that there was a law which put a moratorium on speech in elevators. The silence is oppressive and we are almost glad when we can get off at our floor.

Unfortunately churches are often the same, particularly large churches. When my wife and I first went to the Cathedral in Phoenix, Arizona, we tried an experiment. I was the new canon at the Cathedral. Barbara did not announce that she was the canon's wife, and she quietly attended the early service every Sunday morning for two months before anyone spoke to her, a stranger. In many churches the gospel statement, "Many are called, but few are chosen," could well be parodied: "Many are cold, but few are frozen." One can often find as much fellowship by going to a movie theatre as by going to church.

Some people do not like to pass the peace at Eucharist, and yet this is one of the most ancient and integral parts of

174

Eucharist. It is an attempt to realize our brotherhood with one another. If, however, the peace does not move outside the church into an easy conversation, it is not genuine. The peace should be a symbol of loving care which continues after the service.

I can understand why people were uncomfortable receiving Communion during the Middle Ages. Once the body and blood of the loving Christ was coursing through their veins and there was no change in them, they began to feel guilty. What is our spiritual state if we exchange the peace, receive Eucharist and then do not greet the same people as we leave the church? Are we then listening to what Christ said about reaching out to strangers?

Most of the evil in this world is caused not by wicked people, but by unconscious people, by the very kind of unconsciousness which lets us ignore others. Unconscious people are run, not by conscious motivation, but rather by whatever pops up out of their unconscious depths. Sometimes it is an action of thoughtfulness or forgiveness, but it can just as well be impulsiveness, a bigoted cultural heritage, a stupid prejudice, indifference or fear. It takes real discipline to be genuinely evil, but the easiest thing in the world is to live unconsciously. In a letter to a priest friend Jung states that perhaps the essence of most evil is unconsciousness.

A friend of mine returning from the war told me of an experience that showed him how his prejudices made others strangers to him. In the South Pacific he met and became fast friends with a soldier about his own age. When he arrived there, my friend found his companion to be more congenial than anyone he had ever known. After the war they arranged to meet below the clock at Grand Central Station in New York. He saw a man approaching him wearing a ghastly green suit. It was his friend. The realization suddenly came to him that if he had not met his friend in the service where they were wearing the same G.I. garb, his prejudice about clothes would have kept him from his closest friendship. He never would have given anyone dressed like that the time of day.

175

Reaching Out

Being aware of strangers requires some growth in consciousness. Seldom is this achieved without reflection and prayer. It is another example of how loving action is seldom possible unless it is rooted in prayer. Suddenly some more scales fall from my eyes and I see that other persons or groups of people are just as frightened and alien as I am. I see their hungry eyes, their eager expectancy. Of course, I may not be reading the situation correctly, but I will never know unless I take the next step and reach out with an extended hand or a word of greeting to the person whom I have seen as a stranger.

This is difficult for an introvert, just as difficult as it is for the extrovert to take time in quiet and reflection. (Both my wife and I are introverts, and we have decided that if we have to come back through this world, we want to come back as extroverts.) Thus if we are reaching out, whether introvert or extrovert, we speak up or shake hands. And if the other person doesn't want to be reached out to, no harm is done, particularly if we have no hidden expectations, as long as we are more interested in understanding than in being understood.

And what do we say as we make the first approach to a stranger? I have found that three questions unlock conversation after we have introduced ourselves: Where are you from? What are you doing here? Do you have a family? If people are traveling, they nearly always like to talk about home. If they are newcomers, they like to tell of where they have been. Sometimes we can talk about places we have both been. If we hit upon an oldtimer in these parts, he or she can regale us with family history. I love to talk about where I have been and where I was raised, because I am talking about me and someone seems interested.

It is painful to realize how seldom people ask us what we are doing and why. I have learned a great deal by asking people why they are here. Seldom do we get an opportunity to tell other people about the dullness or the interesting details of our ordinary life. Here again we can share experiences, and as we do, we are less strangers to one another. Again I love to be asked about my multifaceted life and tell about the various things I do.

If we are alone and separated from our family, most of us enjoy telling about them. If they are with us, this gives us an opportunity for introductions. If the children are grown we can tell of their lives and successes. Later on we may also speak and hear of failures. Often pictures will come out and the barriers between us begin to crumble. I always carry pictures of my children and grandchildren with me. When a person is interested enough in me to ask about them, it is a pleasure to get them out and share them.

These three questions lead into a dozen others, and before very long we are no longer strangers. It is as if our two frightened little inner idiots have learned to play with each other and have become divine children. When friendship really begins to grow, we may even talk about our inner murderers, and then we find that the world is not as terrifying and hostile and strange a place as we had feared. Other people are much like us.

Quite obviously we can't shepherd every stranger that we meet. We cannot call upon all the shut-ins and the sick in our community. We cannot visit everyone who is in prison. We need time for reflection to find out which ones belong to us and are part of our bundle, which situations have our names on them. We may find that our task is not so much reaching out to others ourselves as organizing people who wish to meet the strangers, who wish to minister to the hungry, who want to call on the sick and the lonely, who want to visit prison, who want to greet strangers.

A Christian church which is not organized to reach out to the strangers in its midst is simply not living out the gospel message. Every church needs to develop a lay ministry of outreach to the strangers within it and around it. Each church also needs social groups into which strangers can be integrated. Most church services need an opportunity for fellowship; ongoing fellowship is a part of genuine Christian worship.

Surface friendliness which does not genuinely go out to others can even be harmful. It is almost worse to be greeted and welcomed one day and ignored the next week than to have been left alone in the first place. The outreach to the stranger needs to be backed up with action—an invitation to dinner, to have a cup of coffee, to meet some friends of mine who have a common interest, to play a game of bridge, to come to a church group. *It is important that we do not promise more than we can deliver.* Reaching all the strangers who need our care requires more than individual effort; it requires structure. We shall see in the next chapter that some people are called to social action—to minister to the structures of society which often make strangers of us.

One last word of caution in dealing with strangers was suggested to me by a wise analyst. When strangers have the courage to call on us, it usually means that they are in real need and we should make every effort to see them soon. When a stranger breaks over the barriers of separateness and asks for help, it usually indicates genuine problems. We may not be able to handle the problem, but we can listen and find someone who can. The cry from a stranger is usually an urgent cry. We need to take time for it even if it costs us dearly.

12

Love and Social Action

It is impossible to talk about Christian love without treating the subject of social action. The kind of love that we are discussing is more than just personal caring for those around us or for those whom we meet in our ordinary routine of life. In recent years some Christians have put the whole thrust of their Christian being and doing into social action. One reason for this has been the tragic indifference and neglect which the church and church leaders have often shown toward the dispossessed, the forgotten, the poor and those who have been enslaved personally, economically or politically. Often the church has identified with the status quo and forgotten Jesus' directives to reach out to the needy and strangers wherever they may be.

We live in a corrupt and broken society, in a world in which there is political tyranny, national self-interest, war, oppression, poverty and hunger. One-third of the world's children go to bed hungry every night. When we begin to take Jesus seriously and acknowledge every man, woman and child as our neighbor, our brother and sister, then this gigantic mass of human suffering weighs almost intolerably upon us. What can we do to reach into the world? What can be done to change the inhuman social structures and institutions which stunt and destroy human life? How can we move into socially and racially and politically depressed areas to bring about change, to establish self-respect, to relieve poverty and hunger and homelessness, to introduce education and better skills for living, to alleviate hopelessness, loneliness, depression and mental illness?

These are tremendously important questions. Love which does not reach beyond the personal and expand into the social arena is hardly genuine love at all. Caring for individuals is not enough; it is not an expression of fully active Christian love.

On the other hand, there are times when social action among sincere Christians has become a substitute for other aspects of Christian life. In lecturing to clergy all over the country I have met many burned-out, social action-oriented clergy. They put everything into social action and reaching out to the impoverished and downtrodden. It was the sole direction and content of their ministry. This interest and activity was not supported by prayer and intimate fellowship, and it burned out. *It took the place of* learning to pray and learning to love on the more simple and intimate level. These other practices were no longer important. Social action had become the total focus of life, a substitute for the full Christian life. We can certainly understand how this attitude developed in reaction to a complacent church, but social action is not the whole of religious life and practice.

It is very difficult for us human beings to keep several things in balance in our lives. Like a juggler we need to learn to keep three or four balls in the air at all times. It is not a question of love or prayer or social action, but of love *and* prayer *and* social action.

When our social action does not spring out of a life which is characterized by caring concern for those around us—our children, our secretary, a discourteous clerk, an opinionated stranger—then our social action often turns to dust and ashes or even into subtle violence such as ignoring another person. We fail to accomplish what we set out to do and are faced with the problem of meaninglessness when we realize that our best efforts have come to nothing. If social action does not spring out of a relationship to a loving Father who sends his rain upon the just and unjust, it can be concerned only with results and even motivated predominantly by ego concerns. How carefully we need to watch our motives in whatever we undertake. Following the way to Christ is an heroic undertaking and requires the best of each of us in caring, in social concern and in sustaining prayer.

Our capacity to love reaches its full maturity when we "can look upon the twisted features of a fellow human being in pain and not turn away in fear or disgust but catch a glimpse of the face of the suffering Christ and minister to him in all simplicity and tenderness."[1]

Heroic Examples of Loving Social Action

Few modern men or women have touched me more than Martin Luther King. Through no fault of mine I was raised with little or no prejudice against blacks, and I was incensed at the way black people were treated in our country. Over forty years ago I was a member of the NAACP. The changes in social integration of blacks during these years are nearly unbelievable unless our lives have spanned them. No one has been more responsible for this creative change than Dr. King. He changed the social and legal structure of our country, and he did it by the quality of his life as well as by a wise and consistent program of action.

Dr. King felt anger and rage like the rest of us. One morning as he awoke in jail he realized that he was seething with anger at the inhuman treatment and injustice which had placed him there. He also realized that until he could deal with this anger and turn his inner attitude of bitterness and revenge to one of concern and caring, of love, for those who had spitefully used him, he would lose touch with his basic motivation and spirit. He wrestled for several days before he could conquer his natural inner resentments and move on with his program in a creative way.

Unless we have been subject to this kind of injustice, it is difficult for us to realize the rage that can boil within us. One student friend in the nonviolence program at the University of Notre Dame joined in a peace march in Washing-

181

ton. Along with over a thousand others he was arrested and put into custody in a gymnasium for several days. His whole inner being revolted in fury at this injustice—and it was injustice, for he later received reparation for false arrest. He told me that he had no idea of the volcano of rage and hatred that boiled within him until that time of custody. He also realized that much of his interest in nonviolence had been as escape from dealing with his own monumental inner violent rage.

There is no more patent violation of universal brotherhood than the institution of slavery. It took nearly seventeen centuries before Christians began to realize that owning people was using people, and that using them was a violation of everything which Jesus preached and lived. Two Christians did much to change the world's attitude about slavery. The first of them was a Quaker tailor, John Woolman. His *Journal* records the story of how the insight came to him during his prayer time that no Christian could own another. With no fanfare he quietly traveled up and down the Eastern seaboard of Colonial America speaking his deep conviction in Quaker Meeting after Quaker Meeting. By the time of his death in 1772 no Quakers owned slaves.

William Wilberforce came from a totally different background; he was a part of the establishment. He was converted to Christianity in 1785 in Great Britain. As a member of Parliament, he worked for over forty years for the abolition of slavery in the British Empire. He could not see how any Christian could own another. Year after year he presented bills in the House of Commons. A month after his death in 1833 slavery was finally abolished in all British possessions. The determined conviction of this skillful politician bore fruit. Finally one part of the message of Jesus was implemented politically on a large scale.

Some people deal with injustice by taking it upon themselves. Almost nothing was done to help the plight of the poor when St. Francis made lady poverty his bride and went to live among the most destitute, the dispossessed and starving, the lepers and outcasts. One of his followers found Francis out in the cold night shivering and asked him why

182

he was there. He replied that in this way he joined the vast fellowship of those who were cold and homeless and bore their burden with them. Francis so touched the heart of his indifferent age that the church was revitalized and the poor were ministered to by thousands upon thousands of friars who followed Francis.

And Francis showed the same kind of warmth and love to those who surrounded him in the order. One of his companions came to Francis annoyed and irritated by the way people admired and followed him and exclaimed sarcastically: "Why did God pick you?" Francis replied with simplicity: "He looked for the most unlikely and most unprofitable servant he could find so that his Glory, not mine, would show through."

Albert Schweitzer is another who showed the same kind of intensity in his love for life. He left a career as theologian and organist to learn medicine. He went among the forgotten and diseased in Africa to bring concern and healing.

Few living people have stirred the imaginations of Christians more than Mother Teresa of Caluctta. In a place of incalculable poverty and hopelessness she has brought food to the hungry, shelter to the homeless and comfort to the dying. When asked how she could bear not reaching more unfortunate people, she replied: "My task is not to be successful, but to be faithful."

We do not have to go to India or Indonesia to find destitution and hopelessness. Just across the border of the United States at El Paso lies the city of Juarez. Tens of thousands of peasants have fled from the deep interior of Mexico, hoping to come into the promised land on the other side of the Rio Grande. On the barren former city dumps thousands of these people have built squatters' shanties. There is no water unless there is money to pay for it. And the only place to store water is in large uncovered oil drums. The land is high desert, so it gets very cold at night in the winter, and there is no wood to collect. Many people do not even have a warm blanket to cover them at night and many, especially older people, die of exposure.

A group of charismatic Christians from Our Lady's

Youth Center in El Paso saw the need and felt called to minister to this human suffering. Few ministries have impressed me more. These volunteers go over the border each day bringing food, teaching the people to read and write, and helping them develop skills by which they can learn to make a living. They teach the people how to care for each other and have brought order and hope to the lives of thousands of people. They do what they can without being discouraged by the needs they cannot meet.

One could go on and on. Most canonized saints have made some kind of social impact. St. Catherine of Siena expressed outrage at the schism in the church and partially through her efforts schism between various popes was healed. She wrote to kings, urging justice and concern for the poor. She was fearless. St. Catherine of Genoa gave up her palatial home and went to live in a hospital where she ministered to the sick. She and her followers organized a ministry to those condemned to die. Wherever Christianity has been vital we find this kind of outreach to strangers and the dispossessed.

What Can We Do?

Sometimes when we see the enormity of the problem on earth we become so overwhelmed that we are paralyzed and don't know where to begin. One way we can avoid this reaction once our eyes are opened is to discover what we are called by God to do. Not everyone is called to be a Brother Francis or an Albert Schweitzer. We need discernment. A young man came to his pastor and said that he was called to be a preacher. When he was asked why he was so sure, the youth replied that while he had been lying on his back gazing up at the clouds, he saw the letters "P C" in them and he was sure it meant that he was to preach Christ. The minister quietly told him that he had misinterpreted the sign; it really was telling him to plant corn.

What we are to do in the field of social action may be determined by our training, our abilities, and even our type structure. My wife and I were discussing the unbelievable situation in Calcutta where Mother Teresa labors. If my wife were there, she, as a feeling-sensation type, would want to be directing a program that ministered to the immediate needs of the poor, starving, sick individuals. I see the need to get across to the people of India the reality of this *physical* world and the suffering in it. The basic problem in India is that most people don't believe that the physical world is real (it is only illusion). For a thinking-intuitive like me, it is important to get at the causes of problems. The problems of the world need the efforts of all of us, and we need the charity to see that many others are struggling to solve them in ways that are sometimes quite different than ours but are just as valid.

Any of us in an overprivileged country like our own can give money to help others do their work. We can give money when we are unable to give in another way. If we give generously and with love, it can be a genuine expression of social action for the miserable of the earth. Creative giving requires that we know where the needs are greatest and which of the people and agencies that are ministering are reaching out most effectively. Giving which is not generous, wise and informed can be no more than a sop to a guilty conscience.

Some people are called to the life of intercession. This is something that even the bedridden can do. Sincere, consistent prayer gives support and encouragement, opens doors, and can create miracles. This, too, can be genuine social action as long as the prayer does not take the place of dealing with human need when the need lies in our path.

At some point we need to stop and ask ourselves how our love reaches beyond our inner circle of family, friends and acquaintances and out to the strangers whom we have never met. Which human need tugs at our heart? Which burden seems to be laid upon us? Is it the prison system? Is it our system of justice which seldom sends any but the poor and underprivileged to prison? Is it the cause of justice for women? for blacks? for migrant laborers? for those dying in Juarez, Calcutta or Jakarta? for those destroying themselves with drugs in Hong Kong? Or is our cause that of justice for political prisoners, or education, or battling the crippling effects of disease? Or is it perhaps ministering

185

to those who are depressed and have lost meaning in our own suburban society? Misery is misery wherever it is. Christian love with its eyes open will reach out in concrete ways to human agony.

Concern for Others in the Lord's Prayer

Should we doubt that the Christian is called to reach out to others, we need only turn to the Lord's Prayer for confirmation of this conviction. Jesus taught his disciples this prayer, and it contains the essence of his belief and practice. Within the rhythmic words of this prayer there is the insistent beat of concern for others, again and again. It is almost impossible to say this prayer without realizing that we are being asked to pray with the whole human race as our family. We cannot isolate ourselves and truly pray these words.

First of all, I do not pray to my Father, but to *our* Father. As I turn to the loving Father, to *Abba,* I bring not only myself but I bring with me all my brothers and sisters from all over the world—black, red, yellow and white, rich and poor, enslaved and free.

I do not ask to be lost in a solitary, isolated communion with the Father, but rather I ask for the *kingdom,* for a fellowship in which a group of us are joined in harmony, concern and love empowered by the love of Abba.

I do not ask that this kingdom be given just to me or my family or my community or my church or my nation, but that it may come to all the earth as it is given in heaven.

I petition not for my daily bread, for my daily sustenance of body, mind and soul, but for *our* daily need; I ask that all the human family may be fed and sheltered, and given psychological nourishment and spiritual direction. Again this prayer must be backed up by specific action or I run the danger of falling into hypocrisy.

When asking for forgiveness, it is the same: "Forgive *us our* trespasses as *we* forgive those who trespass against *us.*" How different if I asked: "Forgive my my trespasses as I forgive those who trespass against me." Often the hurts which are most difficult to forgive are done not to me but

186

to those I love. I am praying that forgiveness may grow among us all. How difficult to pray this prayer while I harbor malice in my heart.

The beat becomes almost monotonous. Father, *we* are weak and fragile human beings, all of us, and do not put *us* to the test, or allow us to be led into temptation. We are all in this together.

And, Father, we know that, try as hard as we can, we cannot save ourselves from the forces of evil, from the Evil One. Only as you share with us your power and glory can we have the strength not to be swept away into the abyss. Father, protect and deliver all of us, your children.

It is nearly impossible to say this prayer, let alone to pray it, without realizing that we are all in this together. I cannot ask this loving Father anything for myself without asking for others as well. My prayer is likely to be hollow and empty unless this truth is expressed by me in some kind of action for the miserable all over the earth.

13

The Creativity of Love

Love is the most creative power in the world. The results of love are so many and so varied that we can only begin to enumerate them.

First of all, love breeds love. Only as love engenders more love can it spread out into the world as the waters cover the sea. Love is the only source of love. It cannot be reached through will or reason or understanding or committee planning. It springs out of the total reality of the human being, body, mind and spirit. It is both self-giving and desiring. Love that is merely rationally willed and does not spring to some extent out of the heart's desire is seldom love at all. It is, as we have already indicated, only "glassy Christian love" and has little transforming power. One of the reasons for the sickness of much of the modern church is its attempt to fit love into a rational framework.

And then love has the incredible power of turning lesser things into itself. Speaking of the loving spirit of Francis of Assisi and Albert Schweitzer, Kazantzakis wrote these words: "Both have in their grasp the philosopher's stone which transubstantiates the basest of metals into gold, the gold into spiritual essence. They take disease, hunger, cold, injustice, ugliness—reality at its most horrible—and transubstantiate these into a reality yet more real, where the wind of spirit blows. No, not of spirit; of love. And in their hearts, like the sun over great empires, love never sets."[1]

Indeed human life withers away and dies without love. Children do not mature properly, do not learn, do not grow if they are not loved. Babies waste away and die without love. Older people who are not in loving communication with others are the first to take sick and die. The evidence of James Lynch in *The Broken Heart* is overwhelming.

Those of us who have never been loved seldom have a sense of real worth or value until someone loves us. We have little sense of security or stability and so are open to the ravages of mental illness, depression, fear, anxiety, neurosis and psychosis. Love makes human beings human; as we are loved we can begin to love ourselves and to treat ourselves as valuable human beings.

Deep in the heart of each of us is the fear that no one can abide the totality of our inner being: murderer, idiot and traitor. This is the result of our estrangement from God. Only as we human beings are loved and tenderly cared for can this disfigurement within us be healed and be replaced by a new growth of self-respect and maturity.

It is nearly impossible to develop faith unless we have been loved. Faith is another product of love. How can we believe that there is a God who cares and watches over us until we have experienced this love from some human being and are thereby given a glimmering vision of the love which dwells at the core of reality? Von Hügel wrote a short biography of Sir Alfred Lyall, the famous geologist and agnostic, in which he pointed out the cold and unloving home in which Lyall was raised; it was this atmosphere which made faith so nearly impossible for him. Von Hügel believed that God made the human family and its loving environment as one instrument to prepare us to know him.

Courage is another result of having been loved. The truly fearful among us are those who lack the courage to go out and take up our lives. In most cases we find that such people have never been loved. They have never known what it is to have another person standing by them, encouraging and loving them. Or else the love which they have experienced was not permeated with the quality of never-ceasing, unassuming support no matter what they have done or been. Courage is confidence in action. The courageous have confidence in the ultimate nature of reality and they step out to risk the present for the future, the proximate for the ultimate. How do we arrive at this point? Being loved, we assimilate the trust and confidence of those who love us.

It is practically impossible to be courageous—*except in hostility and hatred*, which are seldom creative—unless we have known and have been transformed by the healing balm, the elixir of life, the psychic stuff which is love. The spiritual journey requires courage. How can we go through the dark night of the soul, through which our way often passes, unless we have first been established in courage by love?

And seldom is it possible to have hope without having been nurtured with love. Love gives meaning. How can we hope for good in the future, the greatest good, unless we have known something of it in the past and present? Without having been loved, there is little to look forward to, nothing to imagine as the fulfillment of life; and so there appears to be no hope.

If love is, indeed, the source and center of the universe, then being loved alone can open our eyes to this truth. Love then gives us the ultimate wisdom, a wisdom which is much wiser than the wisdom of the learned or of material success and power.

Love creates peace within the soul and around the soul. Peace is not resting or inaction; it is rather the harmony of all things working together in their proper place. Dante's final insight into heaven was that the love he encountered in the highest heaven created both the harmony of the turning stars and the harmony within and among us human beings.

Beyond happiness is joy. Joy is creative satisfaction which seeks to give of itself to others. In an age of anxiety and despair we hear little about joy, yet joy is an essential mark of real Christian experience. Joy is the result of having been touched by human love and being led by it to Divine Love.

190

Love opens other human beings to us. Until we love, few people open the fortresses of their lives to us. Love is the *open sesame* which unlocks the lives of others to us and enables us to have true fellowship, to give and receive the best from one another.

And last of all, love opens the very gateway to the kingdom of heaven to us. Sometimes through another human being and sometimes directly within ourselves love takes us into the presence of the God of love. Thomas of Celano said of Francis of Assisi: "An extremely thin partition separated Brother Francis from eternity. This is why he always heard the divine melody—through this delicate partition." It was love which wore thin this partition for Francis, and love still does it for us today.

It is strange that God would give us so powerful a gift, such a tremendous power. By loving or not loving we become gods ourselves, for we can create or destroy, build up or tear down. This gift of the freedom to love is a fearful gift. How audacious God was to put into our poor human hands the lives of those around us, and also to put our lives into their hands.

If we love, we create, heal and release in those around us a power which seldom fails. If we do not love, we join the forces of the Evil One and destroy as effectively as if we were triggering a machine gun into a defenseless crowd. If we love, we step into the circle of the very creative action of God. If we do not love, if we do not let our hearts go out in compassion to others and show that compassion in action, then we step into the down-draft of evil which is seeking to draw our world into the dark abyss.

Most destructive people are those who have never been genuinely loved. Whether the destroyers are professional criminals, slave traders, political tyrants, or child vandals, the same deformity lies at the root of their characters. Having known little love, they fall into the hands of evil and express the zero of love, which is hate.

What a terrible responsibility God and life put into our hands. We can either become fonts of creativity and life, or cauldrons of witches' brew, poisoning the lives of all we touch. It is not even a simple question of *what we do,* but, in the long run, of *how we do it*. After all, Satan's real fault in the old story was that he wanted to do things more rationally and efficiently than he could by continuing in the life and way of God's love.

In his letters Paul speaks of love and the Spirit almost interchangeably. Writing to the Galatians he begs them to have a loving spirit. The spirit is a loving spirit and it produces much fruit in us human beings: "love, joy, peace, patience, kindness, goodness, faithfulness, humility and self-control. There is no law against such things as these" (Galatians 5:22–23). The Apostle knew well what modern psychology has learned again in another way.

And how are we to know truly loving people when we encounter them? In writing to the Corinthians asking that they settle their differences in love, Paul painted a word picture of what truly loving persons look like: "Love is patient and kind; love is not jealous, or conceited, or proud; love is not ill-mannered, or selfish, or irritable; love does not keep a record of wrongs; love is not happy with evil, but is happy with the truth. Love never gives up; its faith, hope and patience never fail" (1 Corinthians 13:4–7).

NOTES

Preface
1. Charles Williams, *All Hallows Eve*, New York, Farrar, Straus and Giroux, 1979, p. 228.

Chapter 1
1. C. G. Jung, *Memories, Dreams, Reflections*, recorded and edited by Aniela Jaffe, New York, Pantheon Books, 1963, pp. 353f.

As much as possible I have tried to avoid the use of "man" and "he" as generic for the human being. However, in quoting passages from authors who wrote before the awareness of the sexist implications of this practice, I have found it best to leave them as they are. They make me uncomfortable, but there is little one can do short of rewriting the words of other writers. There are also those who object to calling the deity "he." I agree that if the divine is truly divine "it" integrates both masculine and feminine qualities. It is, however, clumsy and unreal to refer to God as he/she. It is also sobering to remember that evil as well as the divine shares the feminine as well as masculine attributes.

2. Except where the practice of opening one's self to God is an essential part of loving, we will not speak at length of prayer and meditation. My reflections on that subject are found in *The Other Side of Silence: A Guide to Christian Meditation*, New York, Paulist Press, 1976. That book is a valuable companion to this one.

3. M. Scott Peck, *The Road Less Traveled: The Psychology of Spiritual Growth*, New York, Simon & Schuster, 1978, p. 81.

4. This conclusion has been reached by many modern thinkers, by those writing in the general semantics movement, by A. J. Ayer in his book *Language, Truth and Logic* and by many other students of thought and logic. In the book by Nagel and Newman, *Godel's Proof*, we find that the same implications apply to

numbers and mathematics. Marie-Louise von Franz has sketched out a similar theory of numbers in her study, *Number and Time.*

Chapter 2

1. Laurens Van der Post, *The Face Beside the Fire,* New York, William Morrow and Company, Inc., 1953, p. 10.

2. I have discussed the place of story at some length in two books, *Discernment: A Study in Ecstasy and Evil* (1978) and *Myth, History and Faith* (1974), both published by Paulist Press.

3. Arthur Miller, *After the Fall,* New York, The Viking Press, 1964, pp. 21f.

4. *Ibid.,* pp. 113f.

5. C. S. Lewis, *The Lion, the Witch and the Wardrobe,* Middlesex, England, Penguin Books, 1950, pp. 147–148.

6. *The Standard Book of British and American Verse,* Garden City, N.Y., Garden City Publishing Co., Inc., 1932, p. 661.

Chapter 3

1. In Chapters 6 and 7 in my book *Afterlife: The Other Side of Dying,* New York, Paulist Press, 1980, I have outlined the evidence which must be ignored if we are to hold to this view of the universe. I have also shown how this world view makes it impossible for people to even look at the evidence. In my *Encounter with God,* Minneapolis, Bethany Fellowship, 1975, I have outlined the historical sequence of events which brought the Western world into this dead-end street. I have also sketched out in that book a new and more open view of reality which has developed among twentieth-century scientists in mathematics, physics, medicine, anthropology, sociology, parapsychology and depth psychology.

2. Robert Tucker in his book *Philosophy and Myth in Karl Marx* has pointed out the roots of Marx's system and shown how much of it is wishful thinking, heady, fanciful speculation and interior myth. The person who accepts Marxism without looking deeply into its roots is more likely to be inspired by anger and hostility than by clear thinking.

3. I have written two studies of the problem of evil, *Discernment: A Study in Ecstasy and Evil* (1978) and *Myth, History and Faith* (1974), both published by Paulist Press. The reader who wishes further development of the ideas which are contained here is referred to these studies. John Sanford has written a profound book on this subject: *Evil: A Psychological and Religious Perspective,* New York, Crossroads Books, 1981. I am deeply in-

debted to him for his insights in this study. In addition I have written an account of death and resurrection in *The Cross*. The death of Jesus is total tragedy if it is not completed by a resurrection to rescue men and women from Evil they could not handle themselves.

4. I have discussed this story and its significance for modern men and women in my book, *Afterlife: The Other Side of Dying*, New York, Paulist Press, 1980.

5. *The Comedy of Dante Alighieri*, Cantica III, Paradise, trans. by Dorothy L. Sayers and Barbara Reynolds, Baltimore, Penguin Books, Inc., 1962, p. 347.

6. *Death to Life*, Chicago, Argus Communications, 1968, pp. 34 and 37. Karl Jaspers provides one paper in this anthology.

7. *The Collected Works of St. Teresa of Avila*, translated by Kieran Kavanaugh, O.C.D. and Otilio Rodriguez, O.C.D., Washington, D.C., ICS Publications, Institute of Carmelite Studies, Vol. 1, *The Book of Her Life*, Chapter 8, Section 5.

9. *The Other Side of Silence: A Guide to Christian Meditation*, New York, Paulist Press, 1976.

Chapter 4

1. John Calvin, *Institutes of the Christian Religion*, translated by J. Albau, Presbyterian Board of Christian Education, Philadelphia, 1928, Chap. 7, para. 4, p. 622.

2. *Meister Eckhart*, translated by R. B. Blakney, Harper and Brothers, New York, 1941, p. 204.

3. *Western Spirituality: Historical Roots, Ecumenical Routes*, ed. Matthew Fox, Notre Dame, Indiana, Fides/Claretian, 1979, p. 252.

4. *Op. cit.*, p. 112.

5. C.G. Jung, *Modern Man in Search of a Soul*, New York, Harcourt Brace Jovanovich, Inc., 1955, pp. 234, 235–36.

Chapter 5

1. Louis Evely, *The Man Is You*, New York, Paulist Press, 1966, pp. 16, 26.

2. Elizabeth O'Connor, *Search for Silence*, Waco, Texas, Word Books, 1972, p. 22.

3. Antoine de Saint Exupery, *The Little Prince*, New York, Harcourt, Brace & World, Inc., 1943, pp. 83–88, 99.

4. *On Being a Good Listener*, Cincinnati, Ohio, Forward Movement Publications, n.d.

5. Henri Nouwen, *The Wounded Healer*, Garden City, New York, Doubleday and Co., 1972, pp. 90, 95.

6. *Ibid.*, pp. 83–84.

7. Rudolf Steiner, *Knowledge of the Higher World and Its Attainment*, New York, AnthropoSophic Press, 1947, p. 40.

Chapter 6

1. Some Christians turn to certain passages in some of the Epistles of the New Testament and to Old Testament teaching to support a patriarchal family. This reactionary movement is found in many popular books on the Christian family. The actual words and teaching of Jesus, however, cannot be used as a base for such teaching.

2. Laurens Van der Post, *The Face Beside the Fire*, New York, William Morrow and Company, Inc., 1953, p. 268.

3. St. Ambrose, *Duties of the Clergy*, Book II, Chapter VII, Sec. 37 and 38.

4. Laurens Van der Post, *op. cit.*, p. 112.

5. *Ibid.*, p. 79.

6. *The Journal of Marriage and Family Counseling*, Vol. 3, No. 2, p. 13, Luciano L'Abate, "Intimacy Is Sharing Hurt Feelings: A Reply to David Mace."

7. Nikos Kazantzakis, *Report to Greco*, New York, Simon and Schuster, undated, pp. 24–25.

Chapter 7

1. Two excellent books have been written on the Biblical view of sexuality. Donald Goergen discusses the subject in his book, *The Sexual Celibate*, New York, Seabury, 1975, and Stephen Sapp in *Sexuality, the Bible and Science*, Philadelphia, Fortress, 1977.

2. *Augustine, The Good of Marriage*, Vol. 27 of the *Fathers of the Church*, Washington, D.C., The Catholic University of America Press, 1957, chapters 3 and 7. Donald Goergen provides an excellent study of Augustine's view in Chapter 1 of *The Sexual Celibate*.

3. Adolf Guggenbuhl-Craig, *Marriage: Dead or Alive*, Irving, Texas, Spring Publications, 1978, p. 45.

4. The theory of falling in love which I have described may not appear to apply to homosexual love. However, the same forces operate, but in a slightly different manner. In the homosexual male, the conscious personality is possessed by a feminine set of psychological characteristics. There may be no physical

manifestation of these, however. Thus, the genuinely masculine in the individual lies in the unconscious and is projected out upon other males. The same forces can operate between two women but in a reversed manner.

5. Alexander Lowen, *The Betrayal of the Body*, New York, Collier Books, 1967, p. 2.

6. A stimulating discussion of new discoveries in sex therapy is found in *Expanding the Boundaries of Sex Therapy*, edited by Bernard Apfelbaum, Berkeley Sex Therapy Group, 2614 Telegraph Ave., Berkeley, California, 1979.

7. Adolf Guggenbuhl-Craig's book, *Power in the Helping Professions*, Irving, Texas, Spring Publications, 1971, is a very important study for any of us who deal in depth with other human beings. We often wield much more power than we realize.

Chapter 8

1. If we wish to read further on this subject, the following books are helpful. David Kiersey and Marilyn Bates have written a non-Jungian study of types, *Please Understand Me. People Types and Tiger Stripes* by Gordon Lawrence is an accurate and readable survey of types. It is excellent for teachers and stresses motivation, and is published by the Center for Applications of Psychological Types, Inc., in Gainesville, Florida. Isabel Briggs Myers has written a manual, *The Myers-Briggs Type Indicator*, and a brief summary of the theory of types in a pamphlet, *Introduction to Type*. Her book, *Gifts Differing*, is the most complete study of types available. These are all available from Consulting Psychologists Press in Palo Alto, California. Marie-Louise von Franz and James Hillman have written an excellent study, *Jung's Typology*. Should individuals have trouble finding someone to give, score and explain the Myers-Briggs Type Indicator, they may write to the Rev. Sanford Johnson, Sheomet Farm Foundation, Hill Street, Ashfield, Mass. 01330, and for a nominal fee he will score the test for them.

Chapter 10

1. Joseph Needham, "The Tao—Illuminations and Corrections of the Way," *Theology*, July 1978, p. 252.

2. *The Collected Works of St. Teresa of Avila, op. cit.*, p. 92.

3. I have written a book on the theological implications of parapsychology, *The Christian and the Supernatural*, Minneapolis, Augsburg, 1976.

Chapter 11
    1. Elizabeth O'Connor, *op. cit.*, pp. 19–20.

Chapter 12
    1. Timothy J. Gannon, *Emotional Development and Spiritual Growth*, Chicago, Franciscan Herald Press, 1965, p. 31.

Chapter 13
    1. Nikos Kazantzakis, *op. cit.*, p. 386.